The Compassionate Classroom

Lessons That Nurture Wisdom and Empathy

JANE DALTON and LYN FAIRCHILD

Zephyr Press

Chicago

The Compassionate Classroom
Lessons That Nurture Wisdom and Empathy

Grades 5–12

©2004 by Jane Dalton and Lyn Fairchild
Printed in the United States of America

ISBN: 1-56976-173-6

Editing: Melanie Mallon
Design and Production: Dan Miedaner
Illustrations: Jane Dalton
Cover Design: Dan Miedaner
Cover Illustrations: Jane Dalton

Zephyr Press
An imprint of Chicago Review Press
814 North Franklin Street
Chicago, IL 60610
(800)-232-2187
www.zephyrpress.com

 Zephyr Press is a registered trademark of Chicago Review Press, Inc.

Library of Congress Cataloging-in-Publication Data

Dalton, Jane, 1959-
   The compassionate classroom : lessons that nurture wisdom and empathy
/ Jane Dalton and Lyn Fairchild.
       p. cm.
Includes bibliographical references (p.160) and index.
 ISBN 1-56976-173-6
1. Affective education. 2. Moral education. 3. Compassion.
I. Fairchild, Lyn, 1968- II. Title.
   LB1072.D35 2003
   370.15'3—dc21   2003011763

Acknowledgments

This book is dedicated to my parents, Barbara and William, for giving me the gift of life; to my sisters, Stephanie and Betsy, for their inspiration and faith; to Kenny, for his patience and support; and to my friends, who provided constant encouragement throughout this project. Many thanks to my teachers, past and present, who have been instrumental in filling my heart with the vision of limitless possibilities, and to the students whose search for meaning and purpose created the spark that ignited this book.

Jane E. Dalton

This book has been inspired and nurtured by so many. There was Jane, who said, "There's a book in us." This spirit to write and teach had also been primed by mentors like Donna Dunckel, Angela Connor, Roma Hammel, and Celia Baron, who all showed me what it means to love one's vocation and teach from the heart. Colleagues through the years have taught me courage and the "artist's way" of teaching.

To all of my dynamic and inspirational students, who teach me daily about love and creativity, thank you.

To my friends, so loyal and encouraging throughout the writing process, thank you. To my parents, Stephen and Katherine, and my sister, Kristen: thank you for loving me so unconditionally.

And thank you to my Creator, from whom all things flow. *"He was never anything but 'yes.'"*

Lyn Fairchild

Contents

Introduction

When sparks of excitement fly in the classroom, when tears emerge, when laughter erupts, when students from previous years send notes of gratitude, these moments touch the soul and remind teachers of the reasons they entered the profession. Those "moments of being," as Virginia Woolf once described them, that sense of connectedness, convince you that there is a deeper life of the soul to explore. This book supports teachers who are trying to cultivate such a spirit in the classroom.

The Compassionate Classroom contains 40 lessons that support a heartfelt approach to teaching. The art of knowing oneself, knowing others, and knowing the sacredness of all life are the skills of spiritual literacy and are vitally important to the development of the whole child. Every week teachers can lead a class in celebrating, ritualizing, and philosophizing. In a compassionate classroom, students can nurture a personal spirituality or philosophy that is wise, empathetic, and mindful. The ideas in this book lead teacher and students through lessons that awaken senses and creativity, foster relationships and community, and value intuition, silence, and spiritual diversity. Teachers who do so know that they are creating havens of peace and understanding that provide stillness and perspective outside the frenetic pace of modern life.

The ideas we present are an accumulation of our own work and experiences, as teachers and as students. We thank all those former teachers who have been our guides and those students who have been our teachers, and who like ourselves know in their hearts that education must first nurture the soul. Teaching is an ongoing pilgrimage toward the self, and as a mentor once told us, "We teach most what we need to learn." "Soul work," the truest work of any education, is a lifelong journey for teachers and students.

How Do I Use This Book?

We have divided our book into seasons because we believe that we must stay attuned to the pulses that were once such a driving force in people's daily lives. Though modern Western lifestyles tend to resist nature, we all still dance to its rhythms. The process of planting, nurturing, and harvesting food is a metaphor for teaching and learning. Throughout history, people of every culture have created beliefs and ceremonies that interpret, navigate, and honor nature's cycles. Combining these understandings, we have defined the seasons in our own way, borrowing from various traditions as well as reflecting upon our own sense of time and process. Though we place lessons within the seasonal calendar as suggested activities for certain times of year, our framework is merely a guide to assist you in determining which activity best suits the seasons within your own classroom.

TEACH FROM THE HEART

Some of your best teaching flows spontaneously from your deepest intuition. At its core, teaching is the artistry of creating experiences that lead people into greater awareness. It's an artistry of knowing the moods, needs, and expectations of your students while staying fully aware of your own. We hope you will approach these lessons with an artist's eye and thus help create them: That is the first principle of usage.

Each entry begins with a phrase or question you might have heard from your own lips or from the students, such as "Respect others" or "What's for lunch?" These words capture the topic and spirit of the entry along with a question that identifies the lesson's goal for student understanding. In the lessons we share brief anecdotes from our teaching experience and a short summary of interfaith, secular, and cultural philosophies that support our pedagogical decisions. Then a concise plan offers ideas for cultivating empathy, reverence, awareness, silence, or creativity in your classroom. We hope that the question at the close of each entry will inspire you to reflect more deeply and personally on the lesson topic. The appendix and bibliography at the back of the book enrich lessons with samples of relevant student writing, meditation and journal prompts, and recommended reading.

Though many times we specify the technical details of a lesson, remember that your unique insight and experience are the best guides. You know your students' moods, the chemistry of your classes, the cognitive abilities and emotional intelligence of individuals, and the tendencies of that age group. Therefore we hope that you tailor these activities to the right group, time, and place, as you see fit. These lessons can be used in a variety of ways and in a variety of settings. You may find one activity works well with an entire class and another that would be wonderful with a smaller group of students. An activity may tie in nicely with one aspect of your curriculum or be better suited for an after-school activity, recess, or field trip. We cannot guarantee that the activities will work for all students at all times; they will work only when the teacher as artist feels ready. Trust your inner voice. If fear is stronger than faith regarding a particular lesson, wait until you are ready. The art that you and your students are creating must emerge at a pace suited to your classroom community.

RESPECT THE DIVERSITY OR LACK OF SPIRITUAL TRADITIONS IN YOUR CLASSROOM

This book often references interfaith traditions as sources for the philosophy behind the activities. We believe such nuggets enrich everyone's learning, but they are by no means suggestions for teachers or students to emphasize certain spiritual traditions. We are not promoting one spiritual tradition over another; we are not saying that all faiths are equal; we are not condemning atheism or

> To educate yourself about major world faiths unfamiliar to you, pick up *How Do You Spell God?* by Rabbi Marc Gellman and Monsignor Thomas Hartman. It is a quick, witty, and sensitive introduction to these faiths, written for students.

agnosticism. Such pronouncements are not our vision of the educator's role. Instead, any references to spiritual traditions are included here to assist you in opening hearts and minds to appreciate and better understand the diversity of world wisdom and humanity's search for meaning. If you choose to reference a particular tradition when speaking to a class, you might invite students who are knowledgeable to elaborate, while reminding everyone that each student offers just one perspective on the belief system and should not be considered its only representative. Often the tone of the teacher makes all the difference in avoiding stereotypes and misunderstanding. If we approach other belief systems with respect, humility, and curiosity, our students will more readily step up to expand their own awareness.

You can give space and respect to those who do not claim any particular beliefs by encouraging students to find common values. You do not have to define soul or spirituality for students but can let them offer definitions. As Charlie Knight of the Ute says, "Everyone got to find the right path. You can't see it so it's hard to find. No one can show you."

ESTABLISH THE FOUNDATIONS

Universal values of love and respect exist across all cultures. Teachers must strive in today's classrooms to remind students of that cultural heritage. Without that foundation, emotional safety is tenuous at best within the classroom. Without emotional safety, no one will take the risk of exploring inner life within a group. Use whatever methods you find successful in building a community. We recommend such activities as We're All in This Together (p. 6), Respect Others (p. 129), or What's Your Name? (p. 10). Taking the time to form relationships at the start of a school term saves you days and weeks of later struggle with students whom you don't know. The more your students know and trust one another, the more likely they are to open themselves up to you and the class in search of soul.

CULTIVATE YOUR SPIRITUAL LIFE

Make time for soulfulness within your own life. Allow yourself time for self-renewal, be it walking in the woods, sitting quietly, listening to music, praying, meditating, or sharing time with people you love. Fill your own heart with gratitude, joy, and peace, and your contentment will naturally radiate to others.

Autumn

Delicious autumn! My very soul is wedded to it, and if I were a bird I would fly about the earth seeking successive autumns.

—George Eliot

LESSON 1
The Leaves Are Falling!

Autumn/Fall Equinox

How can I honor this season in my classroom?

Every leaf speaks bliss to me
Fluttering from the autumn tree.

—Emily Brontë

One crisp, windy autumn day, I took my students outside. They shivered and huddled together in the remains of summer sunshine, composition notebooks in hand. I asked them to write down their feelings about the season. Here is what Lindsey wrote:

"Autumn, a time of golden leaves, morning frosts, and your breath dangling in the air. Autumn, a time of Saturday parades and craft fairs, books returned late to the library, and red oak church doors. A time of pumpkins on courthouse steps, markets on gravel parking lots, bikes slipping silently down winding river trails. The time of year when everything screams with change. A season in between

where the trees are red and the grass is tipped with golden streaks of autumn sunshine. Where flowers wait, fighting for the last glimpse of summer's heat. But leaves give up quickly, eager to find the soft ground . . . Only in autumn can a field compete with an arcade for children's afternoons. Only in autumn will a tire swing be chosen over a rollercoaster and a car be passed up for a bike . . . In autumn your dreams run wild and free, over land and sea, mountains, forests, earth and heaven. In autumn you see how really life should be."

CULTURAL PHILOSOPHIES

Throughout history, cultures around the world have described the seasons with poetic personality and power. Autumn is no exception. John Keats's poem "To Autumn" paints a lush, sensory portrait of the season as a creature drowsing among fragrant harvests and burgeoning mists. Greco-Roman imagery pictured autumn as Dionysus, Bacchus, or Hora, a figure laden with cornucopia, especially grapes. Traditional Chinese symbols are the white tiger, ky-lin (a unicornlike figure that protects the West), the red maple tree, the chrysanthemum, and the color white. For some cultures, the season also represents the third age of humanity, a season of maturity. It is a time of fire, one of the four elements that consumes in preparation for a renaissance. As the first leaf turns a brilliant shade of rust, or that smoky scent of burning logs wafts over to us on a crisp breeze, autumn signals the end of summer and the advent of winter. It is a season with an identity in the cusp of two others, with the warmth of the past teasing us one day, only to be chased away by sharp insights into the coming cold. Autumn reminds us to prepare for the winter months ahead by storing and planning for our needs. We can see animals scurrying about, gathering food for the long winter. Nature sheds her leaves and goes into hibernation. In these ways autumn beckons to us, heralding a time of going inward, of contemplation. We muse over our summer's end, seeing the harvest that we have sown in earlier times. When we glean the abundance of the season, we reap the truth of our lives. Thus this time can be a reverent and reflective experience; as John Logan once said, autumn is "the Sabbath of the year."

Clare Gibson's book *Signs and Symbols* is a rich resource of the cultural significances behind the seasons, numbers, and other symbolic objects.

LESSON IDEAS

1. Celebrate the seasonal change by honoring the beauty of autumn. Ask students to share what they like about nature in the fall and what they like about the pattern of their lives during this time. Try using the following questions as starting points for the discussion:

   - How is autumn reflected in your life? In what ways have your routines, rituals, and diet changed?
   - In the yearly cycle, what does autumn bring forth for you emotionally and spiritually: feelings, thoughts, dreams, concerns, regrets, resolutions?
   - What does autumn symbolize to you?
   - What special ways do you know of to celebrate the season?
   - What season best describes you and why?

2. Allow students to reflect on the season through dialogue or journal writing, using some of the quotations on page 5. You can also post these in the classroom throughout the season.

> *I absolutely love autumn. I guess you could say fall is like my old best friend that I see once every year. We share and swap old stories while creating new ones.*
>
> —Bonnye, 10th grader

Winter is an etching, spring a watercolor, summer an oil painting and autumn a mosaic of them all.

—Stanley Horowitz

Tears, idle tears,
I know not what they mean,
Tears from the depth of some divine despair,
Rise in the heart and gather in the eyes,
In looking on the happy autumn fields,
And thinking of the days that are no more.

—Alfred, Lord Tennyson

No Spring nor Summer Beauty hath such grace
As I have seen in one Autumnal face.

—John Donne

I saw old autumn in the misty morn
Stand shadowless like silence, listening
To silence.

—Thomas Hood

Change is a measure of time and, in the autumn, time seems speeded up. What was is not and never again will be; what is is change.

—Edwin Way Teale

Autumn is a second spring when every leaf's a flower.

—Albert Camus

Reflection

What does this season mean to me?

Morality

How do I establish the moral foundation of my classroom?

All sects are different, because they come from men; morality is everywhere the same, because it comes from God.

—Voltaire

The Golden Rule, stated so powerfully across time and place in many cultures, became the unspoken standard of a diversity workshop I once attended. The facilitator asked us to claim our "identities" with one or more affinity groups. Each of us stood whenever the facilitator listed a race, ethnicity, religious belief, economic status, or birth order that we felt represented us. Then we grouped ourselves according to other descriptions that we felt had not yet been recognized: as parents of adopted children, as artists, as singles, as African American mothers. Each group developed two lists: What We Never Want Said about Our Group and What We Do Want Said about Our Group. As we moved in and out of various clusters for discussion, the underlying truth shone like a golden thread linking us across our differences: We all wanted to be heard, and we all wanted to be respected.

As students pour into my classroom at the beginning of the year, many of them can recite to me the Golden Rule. Most of them have heard it growing up in any one of the diverse cultural groups reflected in today's schools, such as those listed in the box below.

African (traditional religions): *One going to take a pointed stick to pinch a baby bird should first try it on himself to feel how it hurts.*

—Yoruba Proverb, Nigeria

Buddhist: *Hurt not others in ways that you yourself would find hurtful.*

—Udanavarga 5:18

Christian: *As ye would that men should do to you, do ye also to them likewise.*

—Luke 6:31, King James version

Hindu: *Do not to others what ye do not wish done to yourself. This is the whole Dharma; heed it well.*

—The Song Celestial 2:65

Jainist: *A man should wander about treating all creatures as he himself would be treated.*

—Sutrakritanga 1.11.33

Jewish: *What is hateful to you, do not do to your neighbor; that is the entire Torah; the rest is commentary; go learn it.*

—Babylonian Talmud, Shabbat 31a

Muslim: *No one of you is a believer until you desire for another that which you desire for yourself.*

—The Sunnah (from the Hadith)

CULTURAL PHILOSOPHIES

Many nonreligious groups also create frameworks for leading ethical lives. Deists, atheists, and humanists—with famous ancestors such as Voltaire, Jefferson, Washington, and Lincoln—have a profound love of nature and regard for all life. The Secular Humanists' Statement of Principles (Morton 2001, 48) supports human rights, freedom of expression, and "common moral decencies: altruism, integrity, honesty, truthfulness, responsibility." As writer C. S. Lewis aptly notes in *Mere*

Christianity (1996), within each human is a belief in "a real Right and Wrong." He adds, "Men have differed as regards what people you ought to be unselfish to—whether it was only your own family, or your fellow countrymen, or everyone. But they have always agreed that you ought not to put yourself first. Selfishness has never been admired" (19).

LESSON IDEAS

1. Despite their knowledge of the Golden Rule, many students enter a classroom with defenses that could spark conflict. The first days of school provide an opportunity to make a symbolic statement about your expectation of respect. You might do so by telling your students that the class cannot be emotionally or physically safe unless everyone constantly practices respect. State how crucial it is to be conscious of our smallest acts because these are the places where fairness, justice, and unselfishness begin.

2. Display the list of Golden Rule quotations for all to read, without the religious and cultural affiliations included and without referring to the phrase "the Golden Rule." Ask students to read each statement aloud, then guess which religion or culture might have expressed such a thought. This process will educate you about students' prior knowledge, including their spiritual traditions. Once their ideas are exhausted, reveal each affiliation.

3. Ask students, "What is the point or theme reflected in all these quotations?" They will see how the same idea—the Golden Rule—has emerged in multiple cultures.

4. Ask students to make lists of the specific ways in which they want to be treated as well as the specific ways in which they would like to treat others. You can model with an example of your own. Begin statements with the phrase, "I would like to . . ." and follow with a second statement, "I would like others to . . ." Students may write these wishes

American artist Norman Rockwell's 1961 painting *The Golden Rule* is an excellent visual accompaniment to these quotations. It depicts a multiplicity of faiths—such as Christians and Hindus, Muslims and Jews, Buddhists and Shintoists—gathered around the words, "Do unto others as you would have them do unto you."

anonymously on index cards at home or within the classroom, depending on the comfort level of your group. Some of my students wrote:

- I like other people to respect my decisions and opinions.
- I would like everyone not to judge people by their appearance.
- When someone is commenting or asking a question, I should pay attention.
- I wish I could be gentler with those who are having hard times.
- I want to be more understanding of other people.

5. For homework, you might ask students to choose one of the Golden Rule quotations and reflect on why that particular wording is effective and inspirational in communicating this universal value. Students can also be encouraged to ask family members for other cultural proverbs and spiritual text that express the same theme, and to bring these back to class to share.

6. One particular time I asked my students to decorate pockets (former library cardholders that had been discarded) to serve as receptacles for the cards they had created. I attached the pockets to a poster reading "The Golden Rule" and depicting a ruler. The poster remained on the wall so that anyone could read the cards throughout the year. This lesson is a beginning in the process of cultivating respect.

> *Being all fashioned of the self-same dust, Let us be merciful as well as just.*
> —Henry Wadsworth Longfellow

Reflection

What is the moral foundation of my classroom?

What's Your Name?

Identity

How can I celebrate the names of my students?

In English my name means hope. In Spanish it means too many letters. It means sadness, it means waiting. It is like the number nine. A muddy color. It is the Mexican records my father plays on Sunday mornings when he is shaving, songs like sobbing . . .

At school they say my name funny as if the syllables were made out of tin and hurt the roof of your mouth. But in Spanish my name is made out of a softer something, like silver.

—Esperanza in *The House on Mango Street*

My ancestors on my mother's side were German-Russian immigrants to the United States. When I hear the name Schlegel, it brings to mind not only the literal meaning of "hammer" but also the image of hard-working, sunburned farmers coaxing crops out of the midwestern soil. They had escaped Russia just before the Bolshevik Revolution, abandoning a comfortable life along the Volga River to make a living growing sugar beets in America.

The name also conjures up the picture of my grandmother with her German accent and knee-high socks, mocked by her American classmates for being "different" during the early part of the 20th century. Her name was most likely the subject of derision. She left school after the eighth grade and later abandoned her name for the Italian Fuoco when she married another immigrant. Today all these maiden names are lost when my surname is spoken, but my grandmother's first name, Katherine, is my mother's first name and my middle name. These family tales of hardship fascinate me; a kaleidoscope of ancestral images spins in my mind whenever I remember the name Schlegel. So it was with much familiarity and ease one year that I read aloud a particular student's surname from the attendance list on the first day of class: Schlegelmilch. This girl looked up at me in amazement, her eyes alight with thankfulness. "You are the first teacher," she said, "who has ever pronounced my name correctly." Instantly we had a bond that a bureaucratic procedure like attendance-taking had never created for me before. Both of us were proud of and surprised about a connection between our names.

CULTURAL PHILOSOPHIES

Many people in Western societies view a name as a stamp of an individual's unique identity as well as a signifier of ancestry. Soon-to-be parents cull genealogies for historic handles or baby name books for a name's meaning in its original language; some also examine sacred texts for names of saints and spiritual individuals. For the Balinese, a name signifies a child's entrance from the spiritual into the temporal world. Until the naming ceremony, a newborn still belongs to the deities in heaven. On the 105th day of a baby's life, the priest places flower petals on the child's head, sprinkles holy water on the child, and inscribes magic symbols on a flower's petals for protection. While bound to the spiritual realm, the child has not been allowed to touch the impure earth. Relatives process with the child and watch the mother touch the three-month-old's feet to the ground for the first time. Afterwards, relatives take gifts symbolic of riches from a vessel filled with holy water and place them on the child. Gifts such as silver bracelets and anklets, as well as the child's name, represent that now the child belongs to the world and is its mother's child. This day is therefore the beginning of this person's worldly struggle. In their Agama-Hindu belief system, the Balinese believe that a person's life is merely one step of the soul's long process of evolution in a cycle of birth and rebirth.

LESSON IDEAS

1. Tell your students a story about your name and its importance to you. Consider sharing the excerpt from Sandra Cisneros's *The House on Mango Street*, where we learn the history of a girl's name—its translations, its abbreviations, its colors, and its music—as she grows up in a barrio of Chicago. You might research your family name and complete the following project yourself before you introduce it to your students.

2. Tell students that they will create an artistic tribute to their names that will help introduce them to one another. They can consider the following questions as inspirations for their art:

    -   What is your full name? What are your nicknames? Your initials?
    -   What are all the possible spellings of your name?
    -   What is your name's origin and link with family ancestry?
    -   How has your name appeared in songs? If your name were music, what kind would it be?
    -   How is your name used in the media (movies, TV, advertisements, and so on)?
    -   What is your name in other languages?
    -   What colors, shapes, and images come to mind when you hear your name?

3. Encourage students to experiment creatively. In the box on page 13 are other students' interpretations.

4. Ask your students to give one-minute presentations about their creations to the class. You can spread these presentations over a number of weeks. Encourage other students to recognize the creativity and effort in the projects with compliments and to ask the speaker further questions.

5. For an interfaith perspective on names, have students read *How Do You Spell God?* by Rabbi Marc Gellman and Monsignor Thomas Hartman. It examines the various names that faiths such as Islam, Christianity, and Judaism have for God.

Metaphorical Interpretation: One of my students, Gal, drew a symbolic wheel of blue spirals emanating from an eye, framed by Hebrew characters. On the back, he added a poem that his mother had written for him when he was five:

Gal (seawave)
Gal is a part of a wheel (wheel = Galgal)
Gal is a wave of the ocean
Gal is the end of a cycle (Ma'agal)
Gal is laughter and blue eyes

Mixed Media Experimentation: Anastasia played with varying shades of blue in watercolor and marker to show her name in a number of languages. Taylor used beaded letters to spell out his name and dangled his nicknames off his poster like ornaments in a mobile. Latoria created a collage of leaves and flower petals along with magazine cutouts.

Symbols of Self: Darren made a collage using pictures and three-dimensional objects that represented him and his interests. Jason drew and found symbols that represented his name, such as a picture of a Latvian flag and ones of celebrities and legendary figures with the name Jason.

Who hath not owned, with rapture-smitten frame, the power of grace, the magic of a name.
—William Cowper

Reflection

What does my name mean to me?

LESSON 4

What's for Lunch?

Mindfulness

How can I encourage my students to be mindful of eating?

I have such respect and appreciation for the food that's given to me—and for you who have cooked it with such love and devotion. I felt that if for some reason in my carelessness I would drop even one grain of rice onto the table, I wanted to be able to pick it up with the needle and wash it in the water, so I could eat and not waste it.

—Excerpt from a Hindu traditional story

In my history of teaching at several schools, I rarely have had a relaxing meal. Teachers and students rush off to the cafeteria to inhale food. It is a short lunch period, tucked into the school day almost as an afterthought. I find myself trying to eat slowly and savor my food, but my eyes are roving, forever on duty, as a new group of students is herded in for the next shift. I recall at one of these moments a relevant bit of education-school trivia: that these time-honored traditions of desks in rows, bells between classes, and rushed lunches were intentional features of the American public school system. Such an organizational structure was created for molding good workers for the American assembly line. It's an interesting thought, but I have no time to discuss it with a colleague because I need to remind a student to pick up that morsel of food on the floor and wipe down that table. I push the rest of my food in my mouth and stand up to rush to my next class. Ugh, I've eaten way too much, but when I move this fast, I tend to grab at everything I see like a starving animal. I swallow as I scrape plates and walk.

CULTURAL PHILOSOPHIES

The noise and pace of the lunchroom rarely offer an opportunity to pause and connect with the experience of eating, which nourishes our mind and body. Today food is often seen as simply fuel. Yet the consumption of food has historically been a mindful and sacred act in many cultures, where one's "daily bread" is a powerful metaphor for communion or union with the divine. For many, the act of taking food is a ritual for taking God into oneself, feeding the soul as well as the physical self. Christians partake of the Lord's Supper (eating a small piece of bread and drinking wine or grape juice) in a memorial service of Christ's death and resurrection. In the Catholic Church, participating in the sacrament of the Eucharist during the Mass indicates the belief that a person is, by the work of the Holy Spirit, consuming Christ in a *Paschal banquet*—that is, consuming his body and blood. Christians meditate on this mystery while consuming the ritual feast slowly and silently. Certain Native Americans eat meals slowly, deliberately giving mental and emotional space to the experience. Speaking may occur during the meal, but it is not essential. During harvest rituals, food is celebrated with prayers of thankfulness, acknowledging that the spirit forces of nature—the Great Spirit, and elements such as sun, wind, and thunder—are the origins of food. These prayers also provide a ritual that emphasizes nature's abundant gifts and reduces the strength of forces such as scarcity and drought. Deborah Kesten shares these Native American rituals in *The Healing Secrets of Food* (2001), adding that "When you penetrate the essence of appreciation, what emerges is caring about food. To care in such a way is inherently other-oriented because instead of focusing on your own food-related concerns, you are paying attention to the food before you, regarding the mystery of life it contains and provides. In other words, to have gratefulness for food and its origins calls for eating from the heart rather than choosing food solely because they're good for your heart" (Kesten 2001, 50).

LESSON IDEAS

1. Consider making time in your classroom to eat mindfully. This activity can precede or follow content involving cultural studies, biological or chemical properties of certain foods, or certain literature. For example, while teaching Alexander Solzhenitsyn's *One Day in the Life of Ivan Denisovich,* I wanted to offer a counterpoint to the typical way my students and I consumed food. I also wanted students to better understand the lives of prisoners in a Russian gulag during Stalin's regime. So instead of bringing in donuts as promised the day before, I brought in a baguette, the exact 16-ounce ration that each prisoner was given each day. I established a simulation scenario, telling my students that I was no longer allowed to bring in junk food, because faculty had just yesterday adopted a policy to ban all non-nutritious food items from campus. My students' voices rose in complaint. "I can't believe it!" some yelled. "I'm starving by 10 o'clock," wailed another. "They expect us to go without our snacks?!" Most were infuriated. But suddenly, a few students' voices rose up, changing the direction of the conversation entirely. "I can't believe you're whining," said one. "Most of the world makes less than two dollars a day, and you're complaining about us not having a few vending machines!" A fascinating dialogue ensued.

2. Ask students to bring in simple food—bread, fruit, nuts, and so forth—or provide the food yourself. Tell students that you are taking moments to experience mindful eating. The goal is not to eat the food as quickly as possible but to savor the process of eating. Explain how eating mindfully allows a quiet that draws awareness to our senses of sight, smell, and touch. Sometimes the smell or taste of a certain dish carries to a distant land once visited or conjures a memory. As we eat slowly, we contemplate the flavors, the texture, and the ingredients. We can sense our connection to the plants and animals that feed us.

3. Ask students to be quiet during this process. Ask that they refrain from eating until you direct them to do so and that they eat slowly and carefully while listening to your words. You can lead them through an eating meditation or read them a passage from *One Day in the Life of Ivan Denisovich,* both available in the appendix (on page 156).

4. After an eating meditation, inquire what the experience was like and whether it was any different than students' daily experience of lunch. My students felt the difference. "I really slowed down and tasted the bread," said one. "It made me think how the prisoners savored every little bit," said another. "Sixteen ounces," someone commented thoughtfully, "that's not very much for the work they were doing each day." You can follow up with a journal entry. See the Appendix for this prompt and some student responses. When you are finished, encourage students to carry this experience with them to other meals. Try yourself to make time to eat slowly and with awareness.

> *As an eater, I acknowledge the domain of the sacred. I recognize that the act of eating may be ritualized and inspired. It may be given symbolic meanings that are religious or spiritual in nature. It may even be joyous.*
>
> —Marc David

Reflection

How mindful am I of the food I am eating?

LESSON 5
What's Your Sign?

Symbolism

How can I help students explore symbols?

Corporations spend millions in designing and projecting a corporate symbol because they understand the power of symbol.

—Laurence G. Boldt

I was sitting at lunch one day when a faculty member spoke of the fun he and his family had shared the previous night. After dinner, they went to the living room and spread out on the floor around a large sheet of white butcher paper, markers, and crayons. Mom, Dad, and kids spent the next few hours drawing and coloring whatever shapes and pictures they wanted. What a wonderful way to build community, I thought, be it within your family or with your students in a classroom. Their family activity became an inspiration for my next classroom activity. Once the mural we eventually created was posted, faculty and students expressed how much they enjoyed looking at the symbols left by others and trying to interpret their meaning.

CULTURAL PHILOSOPHIES

In his book *Man and His Symbols*, Carl Jung writes, "what we call a symbol is a term, a name, or even a picture that may be familiar in daily life, yet that possesses specific connotations in addition to its conventional meaning. It implies something vague, unknown, or hidden from us. It has a wider 'unconscious' aspect that is never precisely defined or fully explained" (1964, 3, 4). Symbols are a part of our daily life. People recoil at certain symbols that others embrace, crave the trademark symbols of particular companies when making purchases, and peruse the horoscope section of the paper to learn the daily prognosis for their astrological sign. Gangs tag buildings with numbers and letters to signify turf and identity. The khanda of Sikhism; the Hebrew hexagram (Star of David); the cross of Christianity; the calligraphy of Om in Hinduism, Buddhism, and Jainism; and the star and crescent of Islam are some of many potent representations used in worship as people seek union with the divine. In ancient civilizations, signs and symbols were also potent and silent voices of ideas.

Cultural anthropologist Angeles Arrien reveals in her book *Signs of Life: The Five Universal Shapes and How to Use Them* how five basic shapes have appeared in the artistic expression of all cultures: the square, the triangle, the circle, the cross, and the spiral. She developed a study that illustrates how some of us are drawn to the circle, which represents wholeness; the square, which represents stability; the triangle, which indicates one's goals and dreams; the cross, which represents relationships; and the spiral, which represents growth (1992, 12). The rich history of symbolism becomes fertile ground, from which students can develop their own language and symbols.

LESSON IDEAS

1. Ask students to offer examples of how symbols appear in the discipline you study and what the significance is in each case. Within math and science, abstract conceptions and natural world phenomena take symbolic forms; within literature and history, symbolic objects and places often appear.

2. Have students research symbols from around the world, looking particularly for those that are globally recognized and understood.

Look at pictures of cave paintings, hieroglyphics, and petroglyphs, and discuss the meanings behind these marks left by ancient civilizations on cave walls and rocks. Have students report their findings.

3. Ask students to fold up a piece of paper so that it has six to eight different squares for drawing. Invite the students to choose their favorite symbols and replicate them on the paper, using assorted media such as crayons, pastels, paint, and markers. They can also create individual symbols that are particularly significant to them. Once this step is completed, have each student write a descriptive adjective next to each mark, such as "frenzied," "graceful," or "sharp," or write a descriptive noun that summarizes the idea or emotion, such as "fear," "grace" or "pain." Help each student see how lines can reflect different emotional qualities. Curvilinear lines are soft and elegant; zig-zag lines, erratic and sharp; while horizontal lines are often considered restful and calm.

4. For the final step, have each student create a personal symbol that builds upon one or two of the marks previously created. On a large roll of brown craft paper, resembling the color of a cave wall, the class creates a symbol mural, with each student using chalk pastels to draw her symbol. On the wall, this large mural of symbols will reflect your students' personal messages that need no explanation.

> *For Indians, images are a means of celebrating mystery and not a manner of explaining it.*
> —Jamake Highwater

Reflection

What symbols resonate with me?

LESSON 6
I've Got a Room with a View

Space

How do I help students become aware of the spaces they inhabit?

> *Why do we love certain houses, and why do they seem to love us? It is the warmth of our individual hearts reflected in our surroundings.*
>
> —T. H. Robsjohn-Gibbings

One day my sister told me that the parish had renovated our childhood church. I couldn't believe it. This was the space where the saints and Christ shone from a huge, glossy triptych; where the Stations of the Cross hung below vibrant stained glass windows; where flickering candles in red votives received the parishioner with a prayer. I can hear the sonorous Latin songs we sang and I can smell the sweet and thick incense rolling from the swinging censer. I can feel the hard wood of the pews as I kneeled to pray. The ritual of the Catholic Mass allowed me much contemplative time to soak in these indelible details. The church always felt solemn and sacred, yet familiar and safe each time I entered. From the moment I dipped my fingers in the holy water, I felt myself crossing a special threshold. The outer space helped nurture my inner space as a child.

CULTURAL PHILOSOPHIES

Sacred space is one of the many spaces we inhabit in our lives, and to each of us the definition of sacred is distinctively different. Around the world sacred sites have emerged where cultures felt the earth was closely connected with deities. The word "temple" derives from the Latin *templum,* which denotes a land dedicated to a god. Hindu temples provide dwelling places for individual deities, which are sculpted and located in the innermost sanctuaries. Architectural designs of sacred structures have often enhanced the inhabitants' awareness of divine presence. In Christian cathedrals, a worshipper's gaze is led upward toward the heavens by soaring ceilings, columns, and pillars that imitate transcendence. In Buddhist temples, the stupa reinforces the link between the physical and spiritual world like the spire of a Christian cathedral or the minaret of an Islamic mosque. In Jewish synagogues, the Ark of the Covenant, containing the holy scrolls, is the focus of all rituals and is placed on the wall facing the Temple Mount in Jerusalem. Services in early synagogues could be held in an indoor or an outdoor place of prayer. For indigenous cultures, nature has always been sacred space. Adolescents also know the sanctity of special places where safety, comfort, and inspiration allow identity to flourish. We can learn a lot about our students' lives, and they can grow in self-awareness, when we ask them to think about spaces they inhabit every day. Everyone finds a haven. This chosen space has a special meaning and reflects the souls of those who inhabit it.

LESSON IDEAS

1. Focus your students' awareness on space by asking them a few days before you do this assignment to spend time somewhere that feels like "theirs." Tell them to pay attention to the different environments they observe every day, the details that make those places special, and the feelings these places inspire. They should consider everyday space—personal or family space (a room at home or places where they have grown up); community spaces (school, park, city street, community center, mall); and sacred spaces, according to their definition of sacred. To inspire them, describe those types of places that matter to you.

2. Provide questions for a reflective journal entry, such as those in the box below.

Reflective Journal Entry Questions

Some of the following questions are adapted from Claudia Horwitz's book *A Stone's Throw: Living the Act of Faith* (1999).

- What one everyday space is important to you? A community space?

- What do you like about this space? Dislike?

- What do you see, smell, touch, hear, or taste when you're here?

- How does this space influence your moods? How does it reflect your moods?

- How does this space reflect your interests and attitude toward life?

- How has this space influenced who you are?

- How do different spaces at school create different moods and reflect different interests and attitudes?

- What are characteristics of spaces that are sacred? Do people behave differently within these spaces?

- What spaces do you consider sacred in your life?

- What places provide you with inspiration? What about these spaces inspires you and what responses do they spark in you?

- How often do you spend time in these places?

- How do you respond to outdoor spaces? To indoor spaces?

When I read through my students' reflections, I was amazed at what I learned of their inner world. One student shared that a porch swing in the backyard provided her with a quiet place to reflect, while another said, "My room is the safest place. I think all rooms have the power to capture your strongest feelings and store them in the walls, and those feelings will never leave the room." One student related how classrooms made him stressed but that an isolated bathroom on campus was home to him, where he could collect his thoughts and, more important, sing out loud. When commenting on sacred space, a student noted that a place can be sacred without being religious: "My room," he wrote, "is a sacred place to me." Another remarked how "religious spaces have high ceilings, recreating the essence of the universe, towering above and yet sheltering at the same time." One of my favorite comments was the simple realization of heightened awareness: "You know, I just never really thought that much about the places I spend time— but they all really are different, and I do feel different in these places."

3. When the students are finished, ask them to type small portions of their journal entries. Invite them to experiment with typeface and font size to add different emphasis to words. The words can extend off the page, shrink to minuscule size, occupy half a sheet, become lacy Gothic or fat Courier. Find a student who is willing to assemble the pieces in one large collage of words and phrases and let him wallpaper the room or hallway with these inner glimpses. Students will enjoy reading these windows into another person's interior space.

> *But let me tell you about men: If you put him on the likes of a Park Avenue and he feels like he has no worth, then it's not Park Avenue. If you put him on the likes of a Chicago South Side and he feels he has worth, then it's not the South Side. We all live inside.*
>
> —Ben in *The Men of Brewster Place*

Reflection

What do I notice about the different spaces I inhabit daily?

LESSON 7
Show and Tell

Self

How can I learn more about my students?

Your possessions express your personality. Few things, including clothes, are more personal than your cherished ornaments. The pioneer women, who crossed a wild continent, clutching their treasures to them, knew that a clock, a picture, a pair of candlesticks, meant home, even in the wilderness.

—*Good Housekeeping*, August 1952

Swinging from Tricia's backpack was the biggest keychain I'd ever seen. I don't recall a single key being present, but in that clicking, clattering mass hung every bauble, souvenir, or collectible she could affix to the ring. Often the outside of a student's backpack or binder can be a celebration of self. Within the riot of graffiti, magazine clippings, quotations, and cryptic drawings are symbols of the student's individuality. If you want to get to know a student, ask her what a certain item means, and she will often tell you the importance and purpose of the treasure.

CULTURAL PHILOSOPHIES

In many cultures certain objects—known as amulets, talismans, relics, or fetishes—are believed to protect the owner from harm or promote good fortune. A rabbit's foot, horseshoe, or favorite penny with one's birth date on it is not a far cry from the scarab in Egypt, the carved fetishes of the Zuni nation of the American Southwest, or the stones, horns, bones, and figurines from ancient societies. Within Islam, the hand of Fatima is a popular amulet used to ward off the evil eye because Fatima, a daughter of the prophet Mohammed, was known for her exemplary goodness. Some Catholics carry images of saints, such as the St. Christopher medal to ensure safe traveling. In Thailand, people of all ages wear amulets of tiny Buddhas encased in gold frames around their necks. Referred to as *khawng-khlang,* or "sacred potent objects," these sculptures found in specialty stores and markets are available in about a thousand different shapes and sizes. Each amulet is classified into categories, depending on the image, and is cast from metal, carved in wood or ivory, or made of fine clay. Earlier in human history, amulets were unusual objects found in nature, such as a certain pebble, solid pig's teeth, or plants thought to possess supernatural powers. People believed that each amulet had its own unique power and should be properly respected.

Within certain objects, people find a connection to the sacred and spiritual world. Often such objects are assembled together in the form of an altar or shrine within homes or workplaces, at computer terminals, and on car dashboards. In Bali, shrines dot stores and roadside medians as well as sacred sites, for the practitioners of the Agama-Hindu religion believe in making offerings on a daily basis. Author and photographer Jean McMann traveled to America to find the equivalent and wrote a book, *Altars and Icons* (1998), about her studies and discussions of Americans' personal shrines. In an interview she says: "You can tell how important a shrine is because people have cleared away space for these very important objects. The shrine might be dusty, full of cobwebs, kind of hidden, but it has a barrier around it that says mentally, 'Nothing else can go here except what I declare is very important to me'. . . . It's like the fence around the Greek temple that sets off sacred territory . . . What makes a shrine sacred has a lot to do with the intention and meaning of the objects" (Fairchild 1997, 2).

LESSON IDEAS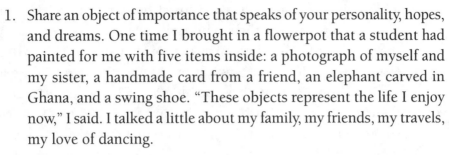

1. Share an object of importance that speaks of your personality, hopes, and dreams. One time I brought in a flowerpot that a student had painted for me with five items inside: a photograph of myself and my sister, a handmade card from a friend, an elephant carved in Ghana, and a swing shoe. "These objects represent the life I enjoy now," I said. I talked a little about my family, my friends, my travels, my love of dancing.

2. Ask students to bring in talismans to share with the class. Think about ways you can link these objects with your current studies. I often connect this activity with the novel we are reading. Once when we were reading *All Quiet on the Western Front* (Remarque 1995), I asked students to empathize with the soldiers' plight in World War I by imagining that they were about to be drafted into service, then gathering symbols of their current lives that they would soon be leaving behind. Colleagues have asked students to do the same when understanding the agonizing decisions made by those torn from their homes during the Holocaust or the transatlantic slave trade. Students quickly make a list of what is most precious to them, and if they can't carry it, they think of what token or symbol would serve as a reminder.

3. Ask students to share in pairs or small groups the history of the object in their lives, and, if they are comfortable, to share the feelings, ideas, or experiences this object represents. Allowing students to share personal experiences with others can create an environment of friendly participation that builds community.

4. Students can write descriptive details about their personal talisman as well as the intuitive and personal significance they attribute to it. These writings can reveal worlds of meaning that the student often carries silently into the classroom.

> Books such as *Altars and Icons* (McMann 1998) and Denise Linn's *Altars: Bringing Sacred Shrines into Your Everyday Life* (1999) are good sources of visual inspiration for students.

5. Students can create a three-dimensional sculpture or altar that reflects aspects of their lives that are sacred and personal. Begin by asking students what objects, arrangements, and structures characterize the shrines or altars they have seen or experienced.

Tell students that this project can allow them to explore and honor what is in their hearts: their cultural or spiritual heritage, their personal interests, or their significant relationships. You can use the prompt from the These Are a Few of My Favorite Things lesson (page 137) or Jean McMann's prompt: "Look in your house and see if you don't already have an altar . . .What would you grab if there was a fire in your house? . . . Find the things that you really care about . . . Don't worry about aesthetics or how something looks. If it has meaning for you, that's the most important thing" (Fairchild 1997, 3).

6. Each student should bring in a box or container to use as a foundation for the altar. One student brought in her Barbie doll case and used the mirror as a focal point, placing photos of her family, tickets from concerts, and other mementos around it. Another student created an altar that reflected his recent Bar Mitzvah and elements of his Jewish faith. Yet another student found an old wooden Pepsi crate; another used a fishing tackle box.

7. Writer Kristen Fairchild, who interviewed McMann, noted that once created, a "personal altar or shrine is somewhat of a talking stick . . . It allows a window into conversation and storytelling about the things that are deeply resonant in the lives of human beings" (Fairchild 1997, 2). Gather your students around their objects or their altars, and let the stories unfold.

> *There is in all visible things . . .*
> *a hidden wholeness.*
> —Thomas Merton

Reflection

What object carries significance to me?

Take a Deep Breath

Breath

How can I encourage students to breathe with awareness?

> *Breathing is the thread on which all life hangs. It is the intimate life force upon which every being constantly depends.*
>
> —Tulku Thondup

At a meditation workshop, the instructor invited us to become aware of our breathing. "Is your breath shallow?" she asked. "It's okay if it's shallow." I tried to take a deep breath; it halted against the seeming iron wall of my ribs. My breath was definitely shallow. "Is your chest tight?" she asked. My chest was so tight it almost hurt. "It's okay if it's tight," I heard her say. Suddenly, those words pricked tears in my eyes. I felt like sobbing. Sadness welled up within me, unbidden, as real as my constraining ribs. I realized this sorrow had been hibernating. My anxiety of the last few weeks had exerted its control over my breathing like a steel band. Moments after this epiphany, I could inhale deeply. The air hunger was gone. This lesson has needed repeating again and again for me.

I first learned of breathing technique in a high school choir class. Our instructor said that most of us were not breathing properly and that correct deep breathing is called *diaphragmatic* or *belly breathing*. We were given instructions to relax our abdomens and let them rise as we inhaled. On our exhalation, our abdomens were to become flat, helping expel the air completely. This approach was very different from my usual short, shallow breaths. Previously, when I inhaled, my abdomen was flat—the complete opposite of what I was now being told to do! Once I learned this technique, there truly was a difference in the amount of oxygen I inhaled. The change in breathing allowed my voice to sing longer and stronger. These experiences of breathing awareness remain as valuable lessons: If I take the time to breathe well, my day ultimately ends on a much better note.

CULTURAL PHILOSOPHIES

Medical research has shown that proper breathing can provide many health benefits, such as reducing tension, aiding digestion, lowering high blood pressure, and lessening fatigue. Breath and spirit also interweave throughout all major religions. For thousands of years, breath has been one of humanity's vehicles to find enlightenment and consciousness. While the Bible illustrates God breathing into Adam, likewise do the Jewish Kabbalists visualize God breathing into them as they inhale. A Yoruba (West African) creation story tells of God (Olodumare) breathing life into humankind. Eastern religions also associate breath with spirituality, such as the Chinese *chi*, the Japanese *ki*, and the Indian *prana*. In Greek, breath is *pneuma*; in Hebrew, it is *neshamah*; in Latin, it is *spiritus*. In these languages, breath has connotations of soul and life energy.

LESSON IDEAS

1. Teach your students how to take deep, cleansing breaths and to take a moment to be aware of breath before a test or at any point in the day when they might benefit. Ask them to sit in a relaxed position and to begin breathing slowly. Explain to them that you will be counting to four on the inhalation and to five on the exhalation; they should keep their breaths to your count. As they

inhale, ask them to watch their abdomens rise as you count to four. Encourage them to exhale completely before beginning again. Once they get into a rhythm, you can gently remind them that they are fully absorbing oxygen and completely expelling carbon dioxide in one extended, smooth motion. Continue for several cycles so that you know students understand completely and are more aware of their breath.

2. Continue to reinforce attentive breathing throughout the year. Encourage students to become aware of their breath throughout the day. Ask your students whether or not bringing the unconscious process of breathing into the conscious mind has helped their breath slow and their minds quiet.

> *Breathing in I calm my body and mind, breathing out I smile. Dwelling in the present moment, I know this is the only moment.*
>
> —Thich Nhat Hanh

Reflection

What do I experience when I breathe with awareness?

Put on Some Music!

Music

How can I celebrate sound and music in my classroom?

Music washes away from the soul the dust of every-day life.
—Berthold Auerbach

Seventh-period English was the assignment that no teacher wanted because it usually meant a classroom filled with rowdy freshmen who were not in the advanced math, science, or history tracks. No one viewed these students as advanced in anything, and more often than not they entered my classroom with cuss words on their lips and frustration in their hearts. School was not a place where they could showcase their talents. I had been stewing over how to settle them down to get them more in the mood for class and to act a little more kindly toward one another. So they entered class with some surprise the day they found my classroom chairs in a circle and my cassette player playing the mellow sounds of Marvin Gaye's "Mercy, Mercy Me." They sat down and gyrated a little to the music, smiling. "What's this?"

they asked. But they didn't mind. For a moment they left behind their shrill interactions, the disrespectful shoves, and the energetic posturing for social status. They were caught up in the music and its beauty.

CULTURAL PHILOSOPHIES

Whenever I bring music into the classroom, the students are always attentive. Alanis Morrisette's "Isn't It Ironic" becomes the vehicle to teach the difference between bad luck and irony; Joni Mitchell's "Big Yellow Taxi" and Billie Holiday's "Strange Fruit" illustrate figurative language techniques and powerful themes; Mozart's Symphony No. 40 powerfully underscores the dark and light feelings juxtaposed in the opening scenes of Amadeus, not unlike Shakespeare's balancing act of light and dark in *Romeo and Juliet*. I will never forget Langdon, a disconnected, troubled youth in my class, who perked up one afternoon when I played Billie Holiday. Abandoned by an incarcerated father and a neglectful mother, this young man amazed me by simply getting up every morning, much less paying attention in my class. Listening to the warbling notes of the soulful Holiday, he came alive. The song moved him to inquire after it, discuss it, marvel over it.

Students are transported by music; they crave it and need it almost as much as they need food. Scientific studies have evaluated the benefits of music and have found that it can help in the treatment of anxiety and depression, among other ailments. Studies have also shown that when students listen to classical music while working, their retention of information improves.

> Don Campbell's *The Mozart Effect* and Jonathan Goldman's *Healing Sounds* are excellent references for information on the benefits of music.

All over the world, sound enriches and expresses spirituality. Gospel music is famous for bringing sound and movement to prayer. The sound "Om" is a sacred syllable chanted before and after Hindu, Jainist, and Buddhist prayers. In Hinduism the Upanishads speak of how the sound begins deep in the body and is believed by some to be the first sound ever expressed, containing the essence of true knowledge. Our bodies—rhythmic instruments themselves with hearts beating, lungs rising and falling, and blood pulsing—innately respond to the healing power of sound and music. So why is it that music represents such a small portion of our curriculum?

LESSON IDEAS

1. Bring in music and encourage students to be on the lookout for music that relates to the curriculum. I will never forget my English teacher who let me type up the lyrics of and play Billy Joel's "Only the Good Die Young" for the class. I had realized that Joel's song directly paralleled our study of the 17th-century English poets trying to entice young ladies into romance with the message of *carpe diem*. To this day, my memories of the literary period and this music are inextricably intertwined.

2. Invite students to see how dance and music can be used to bring to life everything from literature to the quadratic formula:

   - Open-ended projects, such as "Respond to this piece of literature using music" or "Give this mathematical principle its own soundtrack" can reveal students' amazing talents when they invent songs and dances.
   - Cultural boundaries can disappear when history or foreign-language teachers showcase popular music from around the world. Encourage students to notice similarities in rhythm as well as the different sounds created by unfamiliar instruments. Print out translations of popular songs in foreign languages, leaving out certain words. As students follow along, they will have to listen attentively for the word as well as determine the meaning through context.

3. Try integrating rhythm and music into daily activities. If your class needs a little inspiration and waking up one day, ask students to get in twos or threes and become a percussion team, using their bodies. Slapping knees, tapping or stomping feet, and clicking tongues are just some of the many instrument options. Tell them that their task is to tap out a well-known nursery rhyme tune such as "Row, Row, Row Your Boat" or "Mary Had a Little Lamb" and see if others can recognize the tune. Then see if one student can start a round and get others to recognize the rhythm and then join in as one unit.

4. Students can create their own instruments in art or music classes, using clay for drums, copper pipes for flutes, and found objects and clay for chimes. Instruments from around the world can inspire

students in their creations. American traditional music, such as bluegrass or Appalachian folk, provides ready models with their "found" instruments, such as washboards and kettles.

> Let music play in your classroom as students enter and as they work. See how different types of music can enrich and transform the atmosphere.

5. Invite students to bring in music and to listen to a variety of sounds: Classical, jazz, blues, rock, gospel, hip hop, folk, reggae, country, world, and new age provide a spectrum of sounds. Play examples of music that might stimulate creative thoughts and expressions of sounds in students.

6. Invite students to identify their emotions as they listen attentively and silently. Then they should imagine how their emotions would appear as lines on paper and draw them using a variety of media. Chalk pastel works nicely when the mood is soft or bold; zigzag lines made with a wide marker can represent music that has an edge and strong beat; watercolors and brushes can mimic the sounds of ethereal music. Afterwards, discuss with students the variety of emotions that music inspires.

> *Music attracts the angels of the universe.*
> —Bob Dylan

Reflection

What music helps me celebrate?

LESSON 10

OK, You Can Have an Extension

Grace

How can I help my students understand the concept of grace?

"What is grace?" was asked of an old colored man, who, for over forty years, had been a slave. "Grace," he replied, "is what I should call giving something for nothing."

—Tryon Edwards

I had just corralled a group of challenging students to start the next scene of the play I was directing, but I couldn't find Maurice. Muttering under my breath, I went on the hunt for him. I had worked alongside these kids enough to know about the daily fires that raged in their lives: probation officers, parents on drugs, and pregnancy. Yet it was hard to stay patient with them when they lashed out unpredictably at me or sabotaged our play with absenteeism and irresponsible behavior. *Why am I doing this?* I asked myself every night. *Because they need this play so badly* came the inevitable answer in my heart. These were amazing actors, every last one of them. Despite having some of the lowest reading scores in the school, they were suddenly memorizing pages and pages of a script. This play meant something to them that no other academic assignment did. If I gave up, I would be just another adult in a string of naysayers, like one of my less-than-tolerant colleagues who had remarked to me, "The year these kids were born was the year that all the trash in our town had kids." How could I abandon them? But how could I not throttle them, either? Because now Maurice was missing in action, again, and it was his cue. Finally, I found him: in the back of the cafeteria, stealing cookies from the kitchen. I stared at him in disbelief, and he stared back at me, shocked at being discovered. "Maurice," I said finally, when words had found me, "are you hungry?" He hung his head, sheepish. "No, ma'am," he said. He put the cookies back. I didn't turn him in.

CULTURAL PHILOSOPHIES

"You have one favor a trimester," I tell my students when they plead with me for the chance to retrieve missing materials from their locker in the middle of class, to finagle an extra day for an assignment, or to receive any special privilege that I can't afford to give everyone. In many situations, the student is a repeat offender, clamoring for that "1/85th of a favor I still have remaining, please, please, please!" My friends who aren't educators shake their heads. "I couldn't do your job," they say. "It requires too much patience." That and discernment: the art of knowing when and where to dispense grace, those gifts that are completely unearned. Grace is the mysterious, loving act that challenges the idea of moral cause and effect within certain spiritual traditions. Known as karma to the Hindus and "as a man sows, so shall he reap" to Jews and Christians, this pattern of consequences for actions is also understood by many people in the familiar American folk wisdom of "What goes around, comes around." Grace overturns this moral order by simply saying, "You've got another chance." Teachers continually give grace in countless ways because they believe that their students can evolve beyond their mistakes. They fight the temptations of the factory-size classroom, where issues of crowd control demand that there be no exceptions. Teachers often favor the organic nature of learning over legalism, giving breaks now and again, firmly but lovingly. They try to distinguish between grace and indulgence, gently curtailing students who try to grab at more second chances than are reasonable or healthy. Educators must engage in an intuitive dance of sensing when grace might help a student and not simply be taken for granted. Often, a gift of grace to another does not have to be complicated: It can be the gift of another day to complete an assignment, our silence as we listen patiently, or a smile of encouragement. Children grow in awkward, hard-to-measure fits and starts: sometimes two steps forward, ten steps back. In the cases of students who desperately need that seventh chance, grace is a hopeful and firm gift that stems from believing in the better nature of the one needing the grace.

LESSON IDEAS

1. At the beginning of a new grading period, have students make themselves a Grace Pass. Ask them to write their name at the top of a sheet of paper and to leave blanks labeled "date" and "assignment."

2. When they are finished, explain to them the concept of grace. Point out that there is no blank on this pass that demands an explanation or excuse, nor is there a section that demands repayment. If they have an assignment they cannot produce, they can offer this Grace Pass in exchange and receive hours or days of extra time, as you specify, to complete it.

3. Ask students to write about the concept of grace using the following questions as their guide. (See the appendix, page 158, for examples of past student responses.) The subject can tap a deep source in each student and an individualized understanding of what grace is. For a less personal entry point into the topic, have students write about how a character in a novel or a historical figure wrestles with the concept of grace, adapting the questions below to the topic:

   • How have you heard the word "grace" defined?
   • How do you personally define "grace"?
   • In what ways have you been given grace lately? How often?

- How did you respond?
- Who in your life is especially in need of grace?
- To whom is it hard for you to give grace?

4. Depending on the comfort level of your students, consider reading or discussing their writings aloud. If students have chosen to write about personal spiritual beliefs, you will need to establish a "listening without judgment" rule. Students should know that the purpose of the sharing is not to critique or challenge one another's beliefs but to let people express their ideas and emotions. Those who read aloud should be encouraged to be sensitive and perhaps choose not to read statements that could be interpreted as disrespectful toward others' beliefs.

> *Man is born broken.*
> *He lives by mending.*
> *The grace of God is glue.*
> —Eugene O'Neill

5. Encourage your students to remain aware of times when grace comes into their lives.

Reflection

In what ways have I been given grace?

Winter

*I prefer winter and fall, when you feel the bone structure
of the landscape—the loneliness of it, the dead feeling
of winter. Something waits beneath it, the whole story
doesn't show.*

—Andrew Wyeth

LESSON 1
It's Snowing!

Winter

How can I honor this season in my classroom?

Live in each season as it passes; breathe air, drink the drink, taste the fruit and resign yourself to the influences of each. Let them be your only diet drink and botanical medicines.

—Henry David Thoreau

It had been more than a hundred years since our area had seen a snowfall of this magnitude. Twenty-four inches of beautiful snow blanketed the earth that morning. The city was in a state of emergency; roads were impassable. Schools closed for over a week, and the main roadways and businesses shut down as people stayed at home. But the sight was spectacular, absolutely breathtaking. Many of us saw this weather as an opportunity to pause and enjoy the simple pleasures in life, such as cooking, sitting down to a dinner with family, playing in the snow, and reading books. When classes resumed, the students were still joyful and exuberant. They just couldn't get over the mounds of snow everywhere. Despite being out of school for a week, kids came into my room begging to be allowed to go play in the snow and make a snowman. "Please," they entreated, "this is creativity; we are making something with our hands!" How could I argue with that? Like all

42

teachers who know that kids must revel in the first flakes and piles of snow, I agreed. This was a once-a-century event; the schoolwork could wait one more day. We went outside to experience the delights of winter.

CULTURAL PHILOSOPHIES

Winter brings seasonal changes and holiday gatherings that deeply affect our bodies and minds. Winter is a time to hibernate physically and mentally, in keeping with the yearly ritual of the bear. The season symbolizes the completion of a cycle, a return to the source of life, the earth. Barren trees, their branches laden with snow and bent toward the earth, represent this literal and figurative death before the rebirth of spring.

For thousands of years, earth-based spiritual traditions reached toward the life-giving sun during the winter solstice, when the sun is at its lowest arc and the days are shortest. The Mesopotamians may have been the first to celebrate with a 12-day festival of renewal. The Romans called the solstice the "birthday of the unconquered sun," celebrating with a midwinter festival and decorating homes with evergreens and laurels. In Romania, apple wassailing became a medieval winter's festival to bless the apple trees with song and to dance to ensure fertility. In Scandinavia, the winter festival of Yule (or Juul) was celebrated with great Yule log bonfires, believed to have the magical effect of helping the sun to shine more brightly.

Modern sacred celebrations dwell on light as their symbol. The Christian celebration of Christmas heralds Christ, "the light of the world," a miracle come from heaven to earth—the son of God—to illuminate the darkness of a world filled with despair. Each week in the four preceding Christmas, an Advent candle is lit in anticipation of Christ's birth. The Jewish celebration of Chanukah is called the Festival of Lights, celebrating the reclaiming and rededication of the temple in 167 B.C.E, when the candelabra (menorah) miraculously burned for eight days despite only one day's worth of oil. Today the menorah is lit for the eight-day celebration. The Hindu celebration of Diwali is also called the Festival or Row of Lights, with one of its roots in celebrating the triumph of light over darkness, or good over evil, as when Lord Shri Rama returned to Ayodhya, having defeated the monster Ravana, the king of demons, in battle. Firecrackers and the lighting of a multitude of lamps in every courtyard mark the celebration of Diwali, while illumination (deepotsavas) radiates from all sacred places of worship and from the banks of rivers. Some African Americans celebrate Kwanzaa, a seven-day celebration of African culture beginning December 26, meant to unite families, who pledge a commitment to participate fully in American society. Based on seven principles called Nguzo Saba, the holiday honors one of these principles each day: unity, self-determination, collective work and responsibility, cooperative economics, purpose, creativity, and faith. Seven candles (one black, three red, and three green) representing the seven principles fill a kinara, or candleholder. The kinara represents the firstborn from whom all originate, who like a stalk of corn eventually produces another stalk in an eternal cycle of growth; the candles represent the principles on which the firstborn established society so that people would gain the most. Both Kwanzaa and Diwali are rooted in celebrations of harvest and remembrance. All these powerful celebrations encourage joy, faith, and fellowship, asking communities to come together and honor the sacred in the season.

LESSON IDEAS

1. Invite your students to reflect on the meaning of the season of winter in their lives, using discussion or journal writing.

   - How is winter reflected in your life? How have your routines, rituals, and diet changed?
   - In the yearly cycle, what does winter bring forth for you emotionally and spiritually: feelings, thoughts, dreams, concerns, regrets, resolutions?
   - In what special ways do you celebrate the season?
   - What other beliefs besides your own call for celebrating special rituals right now? What intrigues you about them?

2. Celebrate snow by exploring both the words and science of snow. In English class, students can examine the poetry of the myriad Inuit words for snow and create their own words and verses that play with new descriptions of the winter season. The Inuit call smoky, drifting snow *siqoq*, wind-beaten snow *upsik*, and falling snow *anniu*. In science class, students can study the work of

Johannes Kepler, René Descartes, Robert Hooke, Wilson Bentley, and Ukichiro Nakaya, all of whom were fascinated by the intricate symmetry of snowflakes. Nakaya, who called snow crystals the "hieroglyphs sent from the sky," (Libbrecht 1999a, 1) was the first scientist to systematically observe, identify, and catalog snow crystal types, giving us insights into crystal morphology and the physics of snow crystal formation. Students can explore why snow crystals form with complex sixfold symmetry and whether there truly are no two snow crystals alike. Most important, students should use these disciplines to further celebrate the awe with which Thoreau (Libbrecht 1999b, 1) once observed snow: "How full of creative genius is the air in which these are generated! I should hardly admire them more if real stars fell and lodged on my coat."

3. Consider planning an interfaith celebration during this season at your school. In Durham, North Carolina, author Claudia Horwitz hosts an annual interfaith celebration every December, through her organization Stone Circles, cosponsored by the Resource Center for Women and Ministry in the South. She writes: "Worshipping together across faith lines . . . reminds us of the breadth and depth of the community around us . . . Our spirits may have a lot in common, but our journeys on earth vary widely. We share something of ourselves, take a risk, and we gain strength in the process" (1999, 268). Her book *A Stone's Throw: Living the Act of Faith* (1999) provides a format for planning your school's own interfaith celebration.

> It snowed and snowed, the whole world over,
> Snow swept the world from end to end.
> A candle burned on the table;
> A candle burned.
>
> —Boris Pasternak

Reflection

What does this season mean to me?

LESSON 2
Happy Holidays!

Prayer

How can I provide a safe space
for the understanding of prayer?

*Your desire is your prayer. Picture the fulfillment
of your desire now and feel its reality, and you
will experience the joy of the answered prayer.*

—Dr. Joseph Murphy

It was December, and the holidays were upon us. In a school with several different nationalities, students were commencing, concluding, or looking forward to various religious holidays such as Ramadan, Chanukah, and Christmas. The season was an opportunity for my classes to explore the world's religions and the use of prayer. First we researched sacred texts from around the world so that students could find prayers they liked or gain inspiration for writing their own. Then we created a large interactive prayer quilt that displayed these hopes and dreams for the new millennium. Before I began this unit, I had been hesitant to approach the subject of prayer in a school setting, worried that parents or administrators would voice concerns. But my interdisciplinary and

nonreligious way of approaching the subject helped pave the way for a spiritual and positive experience for all. I watched my students select sacred texts from traditions not their own and find beauty and meaning in them. One student who normally presented the tough-guy façade read aloud a gentle and compassionate Buddhist text. He said he had chosen it because he felt that the world should be gentler. At that moment, I clearly saw a person beyond the mask: a student moved by a different spiritual tradition. Parents and administrators alike felt the quilt was a soulful touch in the academic environment. One colleague thanked me for adding civility and spirit. One parent asked if she could have the quilt to hang in her office. An artistic endeavor had illuminated the spirit within us to find unity and meaning.

CULTURAL PHILOSOPHIES

Many world religions use fabric in association with prayer, such as the robes and prayer flags of Tibetan Buddhists, the vestments of Christianity, the Torah covers of Judaism, prayer rugs used in Islam, and the dhotis worn by Hindus. Both fabric and art become a bridge to safely explore and understand the use of prayer throughout cultures and different wisdom traditions. When prayer is mentioned in American schools, you can immediately feel the tension. People speak carefully, knowing that an administration's handling of the issue or a student's action could conceivably result in a Supreme Court case. Sometimes you hear fearful statements warning teachers to steer clear of that controversy. But if we redirect the conversation away from religious connotations of prayer and focus instead on the students' spiritual needs, we can find the commonality that links us all, whether a person is ardently religious or fervently atheistic.

LESSON IDEAS

1. Introduce the prayer quilt project by discussing the worldwide tradition of prayer. Ask students to define prayer through synonyms such as *intention, blessing, wish, invocation, desire, supplication, devotion, praise, benediction,* and *hope.* Let students know that the purpose of the prayer quilt project they are about to take on is to explore and honor the human need for spiritual expression,

transcendence, and faith. This quilt will help them understand diverse beliefs. Encourage students to investigate other traditions with appreciation and curiosity.

2. Begin the class exploration of sacred texts by reading aloud a collection of prayers and prose from various cultural and religious backgrounds. I chose a Tewa Pueblo prayer, an ancient Hawaiian chant, and verses from the Sufi poet Rumi. Choose the texts of spiritual traditions that you sense your school community can safely discuss without directly offending anyone or inciting misinterpretation. Ask students to comment on the words and sentiments that speak to them as you read these prayers.

3. Ask students to research sacred texts, perusing the poetry or prose of various spiritual traditions. They may use texts you have gathered or the materials your media center and Internet access can provide. Encourage students to look at traditions outside their own heritage and find texts that resonate with their own feelings. If they look at the words as openly as possible, they can focus on their own emotional response to the words rather than on the religious connotations that often divide people's prayers. Ask students to find several examples of sacred texts and make notes of the cultural sources.

4. When their research is complete, ask students to share their findings with the class by reading their chosen text out loud. Preface this sharing with guidelines for respectful listening and encouragement so that everyone appreciates the unique understandings each of them will derive from these texts. Students who hold alternative interpretations of a text's meaning should feel free to share these in a spirit of dialogue rather than debate. Speakers should explain why they have selected the passage and the meaning they see in the text.

5. Give students the option to write a personal prayer, hope, desire, or intention inspired by their research or their own creativity. It can be signed or anonymous.

6. Make the prayers into works of art. Students can create handmade paper and handwrite both the texts they have researched and their personal texts on the paper, using markers and any other decorative

finish they choose. If you are not able to make handmade paper, any colorful papers will do: construction, watercolor, plain paper with stamping, old giftwrap paper, and so on. The main idea is to present the words adorned with the loving attention reflected in medieval illuminated manuscripts.

> *May my body be a prayerstick for the world.*
> —Joan Halifax

7. Consider making a prayer quilt for display on campus, after clearing your plans with the administration. Each student can make a four-inch-square pocket using fabric scraps, which later you can attach to a two-yard-square piece of fabric backing using fabric glue or stitching. You should be able to attach 50 to 70 pockets to a quilt this size. Each student's prayer text can be inserted into his personal pocket on the quilt, to remain there for passersby to remove and read. Once finished, the quilt can be displayed in a public place next to a collection of sacred prose students have researched. It can also become an interactive quilt if you make small strips of fabric, permanent markers, and safety pins available for members of the community to attach their intentions to the quilt.

Reflection

What is my understanding of prayer?

LESSON 3
Notice Anything Different?

Wonderment ⟋⟍

How can I cultivate wonder in the classroom?

If I had influence with the good fairy who is supposed to preside over the christening of all children, I should ask that her gift to each child in the world be a sense of wonder so indestructible that it would last throughout life, as an unfailing antidote against boredom and disenchantments of later years, the sterile preoccupation with things that are artificial, the alienation from the sources of our strength.

—Rachel Carson

Have you ever looked at the sky and thought, "The sky probably tastes like cotton candy and mint–chocolate chip ice cream right now"? Maybe not since childhood. North Carolina poet Jeffrey Beam nurtures and polishes that brilliant pair of rose-colored glasses. When he speaks with student writers, he shares the revelation he had while watching butterflies: If they were edible, they would most definitely taste like Turkish Delight. This epiphany spawned a magical poem. Likewise, author Diane Ackerman, in her book *A Natural History of the Senses* (1990), celebrates all of our senses and invites us to reawaken

each of them. Writing helps us revel in sensory appreciation and meditate on the gifts we have been given in sight, hearing, taste, touch, and smell. When we search for the right word to capture that delightful aroma that stirs up our nostalgia or lifts our spirits, Ackerman notes that we "paint watercolors of perception" (7). Writing that captures youthful wonder for the senses is lyrical *synesthesia,* which is the use of one sense to describe another. For example, "Violets," she says, "smell like burnt sugar cubes that have been dipped in lemon and velvet" (9).

CULTURAL PHILOSOPHIES

Zen Buddhism reminds us of the sacredness of the present moment, which allows us to discover the beauty to be found through sensory perception. There is a parable of a man hanging from a cliff by a vine, which is being gnawed at by mice. He dangles precariously, suspended between a tiger at the top and a tiger waiting at the base. At this moment, the man spies a luscious strawberry. He plucks it and eats it. It is delicious. He knows that this moment is all he has and that the moment is the only meaning. This dramatic parable reveals the importance of maintaining a clear-eyed, creative vision, that true instinct for what is beautiful and awe-inspiring. Often the frenetic pulse of our society can blind us to the magic around us, and the winter months may dull our senses and leave us even more uninspired and listless. Yet there are many ways to cultivate wonder. The teacher can be the passionate catalyst to help students appreciate everyday experiences. If your students are sluggish and bleary-eyed with winter blues, reinvigorate their senses of sight, hearing, smell, taste, and touch.

LESSON IDEAS

1. Invite students to help you bring in the items mentioned in the bullets. Create sensory stations in the classroom where students can stop and experience each sense. Ask them to record answers to the questions that you pose at each station, either during or after the experience. These activities can lead to journal entries, poems, essays, or other artistic interpretations of the sensory experiences. Challenge your students to "re-see" the wondrous nature of each object as it is rediscovered, using synesthesia when possible. They should look, listen, smell, taste, and touch each object several times.

- *Sight:* Ask students to gaze at a collection of still-life objects you have gathered (objects that range from the multicolored and ornate to the simple and luminous: a flower, a lava lamp, a small statue).
- *Hearing:* Ask students to listen via headphones to different types of music (classical, jazz, blues, rock, hiphop, country, Celtic, gospel, Gregorian chants, and so forth).
- *Smell:* Ask students to smell different herbs, perfumes, household products, foods, and aromatherapy oils.
- *Taste:* Ask students to explore taste by sampling different whole foods such as nuts, seeds, and spices.
- *Touch:* Ask students to explore touch by having them feel different fibers, such as raw wool, cotton, burlap, and silk.

2. Questions for each station can include:

- What do you discover the first, second, and third time?
- What words, images, and memories does this experience spark for you?
- What is amazing about this sensory experience?
- Describe this sensory experience using another one (synesthesia). If this music were a color or a scent, what would it be? If this taste had a texture, what would it feel like? If this scent were a sound, what would it be?
- If you could rename this object, music, scent, or taste, according to the sensory experience, what would you call it?
- If you were an object, music, scent, or taste, what would you be?

> *Develop interest in life as you see it; in people, things, literature, music—the world is so rich, simply throbbing with rich treasures, beautiful souls and interesting people. Forget yourself.*
>
> —Henry Miller

Reflection

What sensory experiences inspire wonder for me?

Put Your Desks in a Circle

Attention

How can I help my students focus?

The Power of the World always works in circles, and everything tries to be round . . . The sky is round, and I have heard that the earth is round like a ball, and so are all the stars. The wind, in its greatest power, whirls. Birds make their nests in circles, for theirs is the same religion as ours. The sun comes forth and goes down again in a circle. The moon does the same, and both are round. Even the seasons form a great circle in their changing, and always come back again to where they were. The life of a man is a circle from childhood to childhood, and so it is in everything where power moves.

—Black Elk

Every time I need my students' full attention, I ask them to "circle the wagons." Desks scrape against the floor, chairs are lifted overhead and moved across the room, and finally, we are arranged in a lopsided oval or some squishy, ill-defined shape. I repeatedly ask students to back up, squeeze in, sit up, move this way or that until we

are arranged in the closest thing to a circle. The classroom takes on a different kind of energy. I always ask my students, "Why form a circle?" "Because you can see everybody," they automatically respond. No one hides in a circle. We are the image of a community, attuned to one purpose, aware of ourselves, one another, and the whole.

CULTURAL PHILOSOPHIES

The earth is a living circle, as Black Elk so eloquently states, and if we stop to notice, so much of what is around us is in the form of a circle. *Mandala* is the Sanskrit word for circle, indicating a generally circular shape with concentric forms that has the potential to draw the viewer closer to the center, which is symbolic of the eternal potential. The mandala permeates various religions and cultures as a way to focus one's spiritual energy. We see circular rose windows above altars in many Christian churches. In the 12th century, Hildegard of Bingen, a Benedictine nun, used mandalas to record her visions. Mandalas can also be found in the form of labyrinths, circular walkways created with geometrical patterns to focus pilgrims of many religious traditions during their meditative walks. The Navajo use circular sand paintings for healing purposes. Tibetan Buddhism uses mandalas as visual representations of Buddhist scriptures. These mandalas can be quite elaborate, drawing the viewer inward to contemplate the infinite nature of divinity, the source of illumination. The imagery is created during periods of prayer and chanting, only after years of training to learn the meaning of the scriptures and the precise drawing methods. The Buddhist temple of Borobudur in Indonesia is an architectural representation of a mandala, signifying the universe. It is constructed of eight platforms that ascend, leading to a circular dome. In India, women in small villages sweep clean an area in their yard to create a mandala using rice powder, invoking the blessings of the Goddess on them and their families. In fact, Hindu-designed mandalas are a part of our American culture. In certain cities, notice that the mandala pattern is cast in iron on the surface of certain manholes, with the words "Made in India." Judith Cornell explains in her book *Mandalas: Luminous Symbols for Healing* (1994) how Carl Jung used the mandala in his work with patients, believing that its symbolism was important to healing. Each mandala is as unique as the person who created the image, thus being a reflection of the inner life of the creator. Jung wrote: "In accord with the Eastern conception, the mandala symbol is not only a means of expression, but works an effect. It reacts upon its maker. Very ancient magical effects lie hidden in this symbol . . . the magic of which has been preserved in countless folk customs" (102). Likewise, Susanne F. Fincher affirms, regarding her book *Creating Mandalas,* "Mandalas arise from the compelling human need to know our own inner reality, to align this knowing with our body's wisdom, and to awaken in ourselves a sense of being in harmony with the universe" (28).

LESSON IDEAS

1. Explain to students what mandalas are, and consider showing them pictures from Fincher's book or pictures of mandalas from around the world. Tell students that they are going to create their own personal mandalas as an exercise in creativity and concentration. They are to work intuitively with few guidelines, knowing that while there are traditional patterns they can follow, the mandala is theirs to make.

2. Have students select a sheet of paper ranging from white to light pastel or neutral shades. Light colors are important because they allow the pigments of colored pencils to be visible. Encourage students to select a color to which they are drawn. Talk to students about colors and color symbolism, and consider using the Spring lesson What's Your Favorite Color? (see page 84) in conjunction with this lesson. The students can use large dinner plates as templates for drawing a circle in the center of the paper.

3. Encourage students to be still and to work intuitively while listening to soothing music, or guide them through a brief meditation, such as a breathing exercise.

> Consider using the lessons Take a Deep Breath (page 29) or You are Safe Here (page 75) to relax students and encourage stillness before they begin work on their mandalas.

4. Tell students that there are many ways to begin. They may choose to trace their fingers or entire hands inside the circle, overlapping them in any direction, keeping them separate, or letting the drawings

extend beyond the circle. If students prefer other patterns, they could use compasses, circular templates, and rulers to create interesting overall shapes and themes that fit within the circular template. Once the lines are complete, students place color or patterns inside the outlines using colored pencils. You can continue encouraging them to select colors intuitively and to use varying levels of shading to create depth and value. While students work on this project, you may be amazed to see the added bonus of them concentrating while working, for the mandala is truly a form of contemplative creation. Often this quiet reflection reveals a person's inner workings in a visually symbolic way.

5. Group their mandalas on a wall and see how the display creates a powerful visual impact.

6. Ask students to identify all the mandalas in your subject of study, both literal and figurative circles. Like Black Elk, they will see this universal pattern everywhere.

> *In working out a mandala for yourself, you draw a circle and then think of the different impulse systems and value systems in your life. Then you compose them and try to find out where your center is. Making a mandala is a discipline for pulling all those scattered aspects of your life together, for finding a center and ordering yourself to it.*
>
> —Joseph Campbell

Reflection

What would my personal mandala look like?

LESSON 5
The Heart of the Matter

Community

How can I encourage my students to fight injustice and to value their community?

Injustice anywhere is a threat to justice everywhere.

—Dr. Martin Luther King, Jr.

When I was in high school, some boys decided to vandalize the school sign with a small pipe bomb. I remember shrugging off their prank as stupid, feeling little if any emotional involvement. As an adolescent, I never thought much further than my own little sphere. The event disappeared into my memory without reflection. Years later I found myself the teacher in front of my own students, trying to address an issue of vandalism. This time, my reaction was far more emotional. Now the act represented a tear in the fabric of our community, one that threatened to wound us more deeply if not addressed. My students didn't see things this way at all. When I asked them to reflect on the incident, a few said: "Maybe a teacher did it," and "It's our school; people can do what they want."

CULTURAL PHILOSOPHIES

At times like these, we have to remember that a teacher's work ranks up there with some of the toughest vocations. Our everyday work is about changing minds, which is nothing short of social reform on the local level. Dr. Martin Luther King's philosophy of social reform was rooted in the belief that we should not be concerned simply with personal justice but should concern ourselves with justice in society as a whole. Dr. King studied how the Hebrew prophets, Jesus, and the early Christian church not only worked to change individual lives but also strove to rebuke the corruption rooted in the structures of their societies. Prophets such as Hosea, Isaiah, Micah, Amos, and Jeremiah exposed the double standards of the legal system and upheld the causes of the widowed, the orphaned, and the destitute. This fervor for social revolution also led King to follow Gandhi's lead in his campaigns for justice. Gandhi, whose nonviolent strategies were framed by ancient Hindu writings as well as Buddhist, Muslim, and Christian doctrines, attacked the British colonial system in India with noncooperation and civil disobedience. This approach was to Gandhi a sacred moral duty, challenging a government that promoted poverty and humiliation.

LESSON IDEAS

1. If student response to a community problem is apathetic or cavalier, ask each student to write independently in response to some focused questions:

   - How do you think the individual whose work was damaged/ who was hurt feels? How do you feel about it?
   - What is the message of this act? What kind of an atmosphere does it promote?
   - What kind of a school community do you want to live in?
   - What actions can you take to help create the kind of community you envision?
   - What actions might you take to help restore the community?

2. Discuss the last question as a class. Find out if students are involved in any kind of community work, service, or activism. See what interest there might be in undertaking a school community service project as a class. Have students brainstorm areas of need in

the local community, such as literacy (tutoring opportunities), environmental protection (storm drain stenciling or stream/river cleanup), or affordable housing (Habitat for Humanity). For other ideas, also see Take Good Care of Your Things (page 80), Respect the Earth (page 95), Go Ahead and Cry (page 102), How Can I Help You? (page 122), and Let Go of That (page 106).

> *If I had a child who wanted to be a teacher, I would bid him Godspeed as if he were going to a war. For indeed the war against prejudice, greed, and ignorance is eternal, and those who dedicate themselves to it give their lives no less because they may live to see some fraction of the battle won.*
>
> —James Hilton

Reflection

How do I fight injustice and preserve our community?

Story Time!

Archetypes

How can I encourage creativity in my students through archetypes?

The universe is made of stories, not of atoms.
—Muriel Rukeyser

One day when I asked my students what they knew about *Star Wars* and *The Wizard of Oz*, their voices exploded over one another to share knowledge about these tales. Using Carl Jung's and Joseph Campbell's theories, I focused our discussion by drawing a line on the board, which I titled "The Hero's Journey." Four stars on the line indicated four points in a protagonist's journey. "What do Dorothy's and Luke's stories have in common?" I asked. Without hesitation or knowledge of Jung or Campbell, students described the archetypes of the orphan/wanderers (Luke Skywalker and Dorothy Gale); the sage mentors (Obi-Wan Kenobi and Glinda, the Good Witch of the North); the villainous destroyers (Darth Vader and the Wicked Witch of the West); and the magicians (Luke, who finds the power of the force, and Dorothy, who finds the power of her shoes). Then I asked students, "If I were to tell you that each one of us is on a hero's journey, what do you think each of you is seeking?" "Yourself!" one boy yelled triumphantly.

CULTURAL PHILOSOPHIES

Modern Western society tends to revere information over narrative, but our souls yearn for story, and our hearts speak in the language of emotions and pictures. As we each live out our personal dramas, we rally to the call of tales full of archetypes. In *Man and His Symbols* (1964), Jung describes his and Freud's definition of archetypes as "'archaic remnants'—mental forms whose presence cannot be explained by something in the individual's own life and which seem to be aboriginal, innate, and inherited shapes of the human mind" (67). In the Jungian perspective, three elements form an individual's psyche: one's ego, one's personal unconscious, and the collective unconscious. Archetypes are memories of the human race stored in our collective unconscious.

Throughout the world, people recognize such archetypes as the magician who heals and the seeker who takes up a quest. Within us all are these basic elements for allegory, fable, or legend; a natural human inclination throughout history has been to paint, write, dance, and sing such motifs stamped with our own original details. When we follow the call of the story, we are awakening to our inner voice of boundless creativity.

> Excellent resources that explore the modern-day psychological significance of these archetypes in our lives are *The Hero Within* (1986) and *Awakening the Heroes Within* (1991), both by Carol Pearson.

LESSON IDEAS

1. Explain to the students what archetypes are. Ask if they know of a story that is told in more than one country, or if they know of images that two or more people have had in a dream. Have them describe significant images, people, symbols, and events that appear within many of these narratives.

2. Ask students to brainstorm lists of enduring images from fairy tales, fables, nursery rhymes, and favorite books and movies, especially the classics. Invite students to rekindle pictures of people, places, animals, and objects that they have stored in their memories since childhood, as they remember peak experiences, rituals, and family traditions.

3. Tell the students they will be using these archetypal images to play an improvisational story-making game, in which each of them builds on the words of classmates to create a tale. Give each student index cards and drawing tools. Then ask students to draw at least two symbolic images. Each student should make a simple drawing that fills the card and clearly communicates the idea. On the back, he or she should write one or two words that sum up the drawing. If you can make models for students, do so. My students produced images such as the moon, a ring, a wolf, the devil, a pumpkin, and a human heart.

> Students can also research symbols, from ancient to modern, that resonate for many people. Clare Gibson's book *Signs and Symbols* (1996) is an excellent resource, with an encyclopedic reference of many signs, such as sacred symbols and symbols of identity.

4. Review the rules of play (see below) with the students. Have students form small groups of four to six people. The group leader is the keeper of the deck of cards and starts the story by pulling a card randomly. She looks at it, shows it to the group, and then begins a story. She will ensure that these rules are followed:

- Each speaker may talk for no longer than a minute and no less than 30 seconds.
- No speaker may invalidate something said previously. For example, a student cannot cancel another's idea by saying, "Well, that character was on drugs and dreamed it all up." Death, dreams, and alien invasions should be used sparingly, if at all, and might be banned for at least one round.
- All additions to the story should be appropriate and inoffensive.
- Speakers should not feel bound to the literal image they are given. A student who has just heard the girl in front of her say, "The boy hurt his knee badly" and is dealt a card depicting "Fire" can say, "His knee burned like fire."

- Play the game until all the cards are gone, or until the teacher calls "last card," which tells the leader to allow one or two more selections to wrap up the story.

5. Tell students that part of the skill is not simply following the rules but listening well to allow a story to evolve. Groups that work particularly well together can nominate themselves to share their stories with the class or to build a story in front of the class. If they choose to perform, place each storytelling group in an inner circle, with everyone else gathered around them. Ask listeners to identify how players validated and built upon others' ideas.

> *The soul never thinks without an image.*
> —Aristotle

Students can create a version of this activity tailored to the archetypal elements of a literary work or a historical period. Ask students to identify the key images and symbols in the book or time period. (For example, Atticus's rifle, Jem's football, Scout's ham suit, and Boo Radley's house in *To Kill a Mockingbird* (Lee 1960); or the *Declaration of the Rights of Man,* Revolutionary hats, the tricolor flag, and the guillotine during the French Revolution.) Students can work in groups to interpret or retell the narratives connected to these symbols.

Reflection

What archetypes are significant to me?

Are You Sleeping?

Dreams ~~

How can I encourage creativity and reflection using dreams?

One night I dreamed I was a butterfly, fluttering hither and thither, content with my lot. Suddenly I awoke and I was Chuang-tzu again. Who am I in reality? A butterfly dreaming that I am Chuang-tzu or Chuang-tzu imagining he was a butterfly?

—Chuang-tzu

I came into class one day, ready to play *The Power of Myth* video of Bill Moyers's interviews with Joseph Campbell, when the students all exclaimed, "Hey, we've already seen this!" My first thought was, *Oh no, I don't have a back-up plan!* Winging it, I asked students to tell me what they had learned from the video. Immediately they shared the meaning of the hero's journey and mentioned several myths. They explained the role of the unconscious and conscious mind. Then one student blurted out, "The unconscious stuff is dreams, and I had a weird one the other night!" Bingo, that was the inspiration I needed. I asked students if they wanted to do a dream collage, and they all shouted, "Yeah!" I was energized by how excited they were; here was a chance for students to trust their artistic intuitions and explore their rich personal sources of imagery.

CULTURAL PHILOSOPHIES

Most of us have had a dream that we struggled to interpret and understand. Psychologist Carl Jung learned from one of his dreams that he should explain his theories about the human mind through a book. The result was *Man and His Symbols* (1964), in which Jung argues that the only way we can achieve wholeness is by understanding our unconscious. Dream interpretation is the key to psychic health and happiness. To emphasize the legitimacy of our dreams, Jung explains how no conscious experience is free of unconscious associations. A word spoken, a scent sniffed, or an image viewed in our daily lives passes immediately from our conscious impression of it into our unconscious, where a web of subliminal meaning attaches itself to the event. Knowing that certain indigenous cultures have a deep understanding of dream interpretation, Carl Jung sought out Hopi elders and African shamans for their wisdom. The Quiche Maya of Mexico value dreams, seeing them as an integral part of life. In Australia, the Aborigine share dreams in groups, knowing that people have different gifts and can offer different insights. This tradition reappears in modern culture when friends casually discuss and joke about their nighttime imaginings.

LESSON IDEAS

1. Encourage your students to keep a dream journal for homework. Tell students to keep a notebook and pen by their bedside for at least a week. They should try writing immediately when they awaken to capture stray images, words, and storylines.

2. Ask them one day to bring these journal entries to class. Tell students to select their favorite, most memorable dream. Their task is to create as clear a depiction of their dream as possible, in both words and images. They should not worry for the moment about the meaning of the dream but instead concentrate on simply

For inspiration, consider showing the movie *Dreams,* by Japanese filmmaker Akira Kurosawa, which presents several dreamlike sequences. "The Tunnel" and "Crows" are compelling and beautiful vignettes with the surreal quality of dreams.

representing what they recall. Give students paper so that they can create a caption for the dream: They can list words or phrases, tell a story, or write a poem. The word arrangement does not need to be for a particular audience but can be for the writer alone. Students can also pretend to be directors as they write scripts for their dreams. Some psychologists encourage people to interpret all dream images as symbols of self: "I have myself go into the kitchen part of myself. I have myself fight with the mother part of myself. I have myself pick up the waffle iron part of myself." For further guidance on this technique, see *The Dream Sourcebook and Journal* (Koch-Sheras, Lemely, and Sheras 1995).

3. Ask students to create a dream collage to go with this caption. Provide a variety of supplies, such as magazines, scissors, markers, colored pencils, watercolors, paper, and glue. Ask students to think about how the collage can best represent what they have dreamed: Would a certain way of tearing or cutting images communicate the images and feelings they experienced? How about the placement and progression of images? What about additions of text and colors?

4. When the collages are complete, have students meet in pairs or threes to explain their dreams. The listeners can assist in dream interpretation by asking questions:

   - What was the setting(s) for the dream?
   - Who was in the dream? What did they look like, and how did they behave?
   - Was there a narrative progression, a series of images, or both?
   - Are parts or all of this dream recurring? Which ones?
   - What was the dominant emotion or tone to the dream?
   - What part of the dream makes the most or least sense to you?
   - Do any of these images correspond with incidents in your life, past or present?
   - What do specific objects, people, places, and events represent to you?
   - What meaning do you derive from the dream? Look over the events in your dream and see if you can bridge them to any situation in your life.

5. For further investigation or a special project, encourage students to research various methods of dream interpretation across cultures or to examine how surrealist painters brought their dreams to life.

> *A dream is a little hidden door in the innermost and most secret recesses of the soul, opening into that cosmic night which was psyche long before there was any ego-consciousness.*
>
> —Carl Jung

Reflection

What have some of my dreams revealed to me?

Have You Spoken to an Adult about This?

Ancestry

How can I help students honor their ancestors?

The dead are not under the earth:
they are in the fire that is dying,
they are in the grasses that weep,
they are in the whimpering rocks,
they are in the forest, they are in the house,
the dead are not dead.

—Janheinz Jahn, *Muntu*

One glorious spring day, I joined my mother for our annual visit to the garden center. As we meandered through the array of flowers and garden supplies, we kept reaching for the same plants: hostas, daisies, and wildflowers. With a carload of flowers and greenery, we returned home and spent part of the afternoon working in my mother's garden.

My niece arrived after school and joined in with her trowel, sitting between us, planting. I asked my mother how it was she loved gardening so much. "Your grandmother was a gardener," she said. "I would spend hours with her, planting and learning all I could, and we would work just like this, side by side. Her favorite was roses. Her garden was exceptional." My niece and I listened as the sun beat on our shoulders, insects droned near our heads, and the rich scent of loam and delicate blossoms filled our senses. My grandmother was there in spirit. Three generations now sat in this garden, sharing in a passion that stretched across years of my ancestry. I thought of my younger sister's rose garden in another state, radiating its riot of color and fragrance, a sensory testament to my grandmother's love for nature. We were all linked across time with our desire to share in the spring renaissance.

CULTURAL PHILOSOPHIES

Numerous cultural traditions believe the connection with ancestors is ever present and a constant support for the living. Through ceremonies, awareness, and ritual activities, the ties with ancestors remain unbroken. Certain Native Americans believe that a person has ancestral spirits, or guides, who once were on the earth in physical form but are now in heavenly realms. Altars are a connection point with these ancestors, and spirits are believed always to be nearby and ready to give assistance, especially in times of need. Traditional West African spirituality teaches that the departed still maintain an unbroken relationship with this world, knowing more through their experiences than do the living, who are just beginning to tread the path. At altars family members perform rites of libation and the offering of food to ancestral spirits, thus expressing esteem, feeling, and hospitality for the dead. Because ancestors are very close to God, it is wise and reverential to seek the participation and blessings of the deceased. The Mende of Sierra Leone believe that their ancestors come to rest in Ngewo's (God's) bosom, while the Konkomba of northern Ghana say that their ancestors go to Uumbwardo, God's house, where they are in the favor of God and even form part of God's being. In Mexico, the Day of the Dead, celebrated on November 1, is an important holy day to honor and commemorate family members and friends who have passed away. This tradition can be traced back to the Aztecs, who believed death was not the end but the beginning of a new existence, and to the Roman Catholic Church, which celebrates All Saints' Day in honor of the countless souls who have lived holy lives. Home altars may contain candles, sugar cane stalks, home-baked confections, and arches made out of marigolds. Photographs and pictures of the deceased can also be found alongside pictures of saints, angels, or Jesus. Many Catholics carry holy cards, bearing icons of the saints on one side and prayers on the other. These prayers become a spiritual discipline and provide an opportunity for people to seek intercession for their needs while meditating on the inspiration of an ancestor's life. Students can likewise connect with their ancestors to sustain a rich inner life. As they write, they may slowly uncover an inner voice revealed in the intimate meeting of their hopes with the images of their ancestors.

LESSON IDEAS

1. Invite students to write a letter to an ancestor whom they knew well, would have liked to have known better, or did not know at all. Encourage students to express both their experiences and their feelings, as well as their questions and concerns, to this ancestor. The following prompts can guide students:

   - Explain who you are: your daily life, your interests, your hopes, and your concerns.
   - Explain who you are in the context of your generations of family, history, and culture that might be of interest to your ancestor. What roles do you play—sibling, child, granddaughter? At what time in your family's history do you appear?
   - What of today's culture helps make you who you are? Explain to your ancestor what special perspective you add to the family history by living in this particular time.
   - What do you hope to give to others in the future?
   - What major events or memories stand out in your life that might be of interest to this ancestor?
   - How do you see yourself connected with this ancestor?
   - What questions and feelings do you have to share with this ancestor?

2. Invite students to share if they wish or keep their journal entries private, because their writing can be quite revealing and honest. Several of my students' journal entries brought tears to my eyes.

> *Who we are is who we were.*
> —Anthony Hopkins as
> John Quincy Adams in *Amistad*

One wrote: "Dear ancestor, I remember the time when I was nine years old and I had to move to the other side of the Earth: from Japan to the U.S. The most difficulty I had was leaving my friends and facing the threat of a new school with new people. In fact, during the first months of American school, I couldn't understand what people were saying." Another shared: "Dear Grandma, I always wish I could meet you . . . Keep watching over me, though; this year is proving harder than the others." The students' sheer honesty and need for guidance and recognition from ancestors shone through their words. Their frequent expression of "I hope you would be proud of me" jumped off those pages and into my heart.

Reflection

What would I write to one of my ancestors?

LESSON 9
I'm Not Creative!

Creativity

How can I encourage creativity in my students?

Learn the craft of knowing how to open your heart and to turn on your creativity. There's a light inside of you.
— Judith Jamison

As students entered my class and saw the materials for an impending art project, I heard the familiar groans of "I can't draw" and "I'm no good at art." I was ready: "Oh, yes, you can!" I showed them a stack of pictures torn from magazines, photos of animals from *National Geographic*, art postcards purchased at museums over the years, and paintings and drawings from old art magazines. I asked each student to choose a drawing he liked and grab some paper and a pencil. "Now," I said, "you are going to draw this—but with your nondominant hand." Of course, the immediate response was disbelief: "No way, we can't do that!" But as each class came to an end, students were always pleased with the results. One student said, "Hey, this is pretty good: I think I will draw with my nondominant hand all the time!" The fear of making art had disappeared as students realized that everyone had difficulty with this task. They were relieved to know that the picture didn't have to be perfect.

CULTURAL PHILOSOPHIES

"Art" is of Western origination, and for Westerners, the word often conjures up images of select objects destined for a museum. Students need to know that each of them possesses the creativity necessary for artistic endeavors and that the risk is well worth taking to make this discovery. On the island of Bali in Indonesia, everyone is considered an artist. The mayor may be a dancer, and the college professor may be a silversmith. Everyone has something to communicate artistically, and "art" or "artmaking" is a creative process woven into the fabric of daily life, like eating or sleeping. Certain Native Americans known for their beautifully handmade rugs, baskets, beading, and ceramics don't even have the word "art" in their vocabulary.

Art is so much more than the ability to draw or paint realistically. Students enter the classroom assuming that when a teacher encourages artistic expression for a project, drawing or painting is the only option. They turn and point to the few students in the room who are considered artists and tell you, "Make them draw it." However, many artists excel in other creative expressions—despite limited drawing ability—in ceramics, weaving, mixed media collages, glassblowing, metalworking, and woodworking. Their work is no less beautiful. Author Sark (1991) recommends that if you want "to live creatively free," you must "do what you know how to do now, and then 'act as if' you know how to do the rest" (19). Working with the nondominant hand will spark new ways of thinking and discovery down uncharted paths. The process will tap into right-brain thinking—the creative, imaginative, and emotional side. It will tap into imagery, the language of the right brain. It will release us from the overly dominant left-brain functions of logic, analysis, and, ultimately, judgment, that persistently whisper to students, "You're not creative." For this assignment, the editor can go on holiday while the visionary runs riot.

LESSON IDEAS

1. Have students use their nondominant hand to explore drawing and creativity. Ambidextrous students can try drawing with their toes. Students may choose a simple task, such as writing their name or drawing a picture from a magazine, or a complex drawing, such as a self-portrait or one of a fellow student. Whatever the task, ask

students to be conscious of how they feel during the process. Ask them to write and talk about their experiences:

- How did it feel as you began to draw with your nondominant hand?
- What was new about this experience?
- What words would you use to describe the process?
- What is one success you can acknowledge?
- How has your perspective on drawing been changed by this experience?
- Think about other activities that right now seem intimidating to you. What would you like to try next that you haven't done before?

2. As you begin an art project in class, ask students to recall the nondominant hand activity. Encourage students to try new media, approaches, and spatial arrangements as they attempt to express an idea visually. Encourage students who are always called on to draw to try a different medium and to play a smaller role in the final product while others spread their wings a little.

> *When my daughter was about seven years old, she asked me one day what I did at work. I told her I worked at the college—that my job was to teach people how to draw. She stared back at me, incredulous, and said, "You mean they forgot?"*
>
> —Howard Ikemoto

Reflection

How can I become more creative in my teaching?

LESSON 10
You Are Safe Here

Stillness

How can I help my students find a place of stillness?

Respect the child. Be not too much his parent. Trespass not on his solitude.

—Ralph Waldo Emerson

I once taught an unruly and notorious bunch of students, the kind who would make veteran teachers flinch. Intuition told me to lead them through a meditation exercise. I had known meditation to work with students in the past, but this class was going to put the lesson to the test. When I told a few colleagues, they laughed and said, "Good luck with that group!" I proceeded with some doubt, anticipating conflict from parents or administrators, but I knew that if any group of students needed to experience a calm moment, it was this one. I began the meditation described below, and once we were finished, I asked them to return to their desks and work quietly on their projects. They did, to my amazement. This group had never tackled a project silently. Even the most active, defiant student emerged relaxed from

the meditation period. He rubbed his eyes and calmly returned to his seat. To my further astonishment, the students did not rush to leave when I dismissed class but instead continued to work. I had to tell them at least three times that the class was over before they peacefully left the room. Throughout the year, students would walk into my room and ask, "Can we meditate today?"

CULTURAL PHILOSOPHIES

Many students nowadays are constantly bombarded with sound and activity. They don't fully understand the concept of silence. Often overwhelmed by life, they believe that there is no escape and that the only option is to continue on at the same pace and with the same feelings. Meditation practices found in numerous spiritual traditions provide a safe space for students to center themselves. In certain types of Buddhist meditation, the aim is to bring mental activity to an end. The mind that is quiet can become free from fear and concerns about what may or may not be happening. Thoughts may flit through the mind but can be released. Ultimately, practitioners hope to experience an absence of thought and therefore liberation from desire and fear. They seek a state of stillness while remaining awake and aware, trying to do one thing with complete focus: breathing, while becoming aware of the body and the environment. By turning attention inward, a person can thus be in touch with her own essence. She can experience a stillness that may remain with her, even within an active lifestyle. In his book *Education and the Soul* (2000), author John P. Miller cites research showing a number of meditative practices successfully used in schools: following the breath, connecting to the body, walking meditation, meditating on a sound or word (mantra), meditation and visualization, and meditation observing the mind.

LESSON IDEAS

1. When you introduce this activity to your students, choose the word that best suits your community: meditation, contemplation, centering, deep breathing exercises, relaxation, or visualization. These words all express a sense of going inward and finding calm. It is important that students hear from you that this activity is

optional and that you do not take offense at students who choose not to participate. Your only requirement of them is that they respect others who are meditating and not disrupt. You may want to notify administrators and students in advance and consider sending home a permission slip.

Before you try these practices in a classroom, consider practicing on friends or colleagues and then invite them to practice on you. The benefits of leading and experiencing a meditation will enable you to understand both parts of the process. Taking meditation classes at yoga, Buddhist, or arts centers, or local hospitals can further this understanding.

2. Tell the students that this meditation is private time, when no one is to interfere with anyone else. Turn out the lights and draw the curtains or blinds to create a quiet, darkened space with no external noise. Turn off the intercom and phone in your room, and place a Do Not Disturb sign on the door.

3. Have students sit quietly with their eyes closed; do not allow them to lie down. Once the students have settled in, begin the meditation. Consider using the script available in the appendix (page 159), noting that the ellipses represent pauses. Talk softly and gently while moving at a slow but comfortable pace, and be aware of where your students are at during the experience.

4. Remind students that a place of safety can be visited as often as they like. It is their haven to visit whenever they feel stress, tension, or fear. Encourage students to find a few minutes each day to experience quiet. To create a meaningful meditation experience, they can locate a special place, find a regular time to meditate, increase gradually the number of minutes (one minute to start if it is hard to keep still for very long), work with a partner if needed, and bring no expectations to the process.

> *All you need is deep within you waiting to unfold and reveal itself. All you have to do is be still and take time to seek for what is within, and you will surely find it.*
>
> —Eileen Caddy

Reflection

How can I make more time for stillness?

Spring

Spring still makes spring in the mind
When sixty years are told:
Love wakes anew this throbbing heart,
And we are never old.

　　　　　　　　—Ralph Waldo Emerson

LESSON 1

Take Good Care of Your Things: They Have to Last!

Interconnectedness

How can I help students understand their interconnectedness with the earth?

Look behind you. See your sons and your daughters. They are your future. Look farther, and see your sons and your daughters' children and their children's children even unto the Seventh Generation. That's the way we were taught. Think about it; you yourself are a Seventh Generation!

—Tadodaho Leon Shenandoah

Over years of teaching, I have observed a number of students who are not complacent about trash. They shake their heads at aluminum and plastic carelessly tossed in our garbage. In one school I taught at, students met for several lunches in the art room to paint cardboard recycling bins in an eye-catching manner. When December came, they hung strings of soda cans like holiday garlands, advertising both the amount of aluminum used in our school and the advent of our recycling program. A sign in the middle of the décor proudly read, "We Now Recycle." Each week, members of the Environmental Club circulated to collect the cans that quickly filled the bins. As their advisor, I knew the next step would be even harder. Sure, we could recycle to our hearts' content, but could we produce and consume less? We took inspiration from others, such as one school that asked its students to carry their trash in their backpacks for a week, or our physics teacher, who invited us to his home to see how he supplied all his house's electricity needs using solar power. These people were role models of a paradigm shift: a return to living in a more appreciative manner that recognizes our interdependence with nature and the responsibilities of stewardship.

CULTURAL PHILOSOPHIES

Spring is a wonderful time to reawaken our sense of interconnectedness, because the season energizes us with its new possibilities. Spring represents infancy in humanity's life cycle. Life on earth mimics a newborn child, while the newly thawed ground steams with life and the world explodes with green in a celebration of renewal. Even in a world degraded by excessive industrialization, this time of year symbolizes hope for the future in many cultures. Western and Chinese traditions use green as the symbolic color of the season; flowers such as daffodils and crocuses in the West and peony, cherry, peach, and almond blossoms in the East also add to the riot of colors painting the landscape. The environmental movement has adopted green as its signature color with the hopeful philosophy that humans can rebuild society based on ecological wisdom. Seeking balance, sustainability, and replenishment, the principles of "green thinking" speak to ideals that keep future generations in mind by respecting the integrity of natural systems. If we can teach such a reverence for nature, we are reminding students of their natural heritage, including the discipline of thrift that ancestors of long ago could not ignore if they wished to survive. Sometimes it is hard for our students, who feel so immortal, to look behind or ahead and contemplate the ongoing degradation of our planet. But we cannot afford to be spendthrift and disrupt nature's cycles to the point of no return. In the cost-saving flurry of schools, we constantly harangue our students to take good care of their "things." The focus is on the precious nature of human-made possessions, rather than on the earth that has sustained us since the beginning. Instead, each of us engages daily in earth-destroying practices. We can all look at our consumption patterns and re-evaluate them in terms of past and future.

LESSON IDEAS

1. Ask yourself and your students to reflect on questions that help them see their part in a series of generations who are stewards, not manipulators, of the earth:

   - What legacy have past generations left you? What will future generations need?
   - How do you want your generation to be remembered?
   - What beliefs and values would you like the next generation to possess?
   - What behaviors exhibit the values you want other generations to possess?
   - What can we, as a class, give to future generations?

2. As a class, brainstorm ways to conserve materials and generate less waste, such as in the following examples:

   - making artistic book covers with recycled materials to protect textbooks
   - reducing water, paper, and food consumption and waste
   - carpooling and reducing idling at drive-through windows

3. Plan a project together that contributes to the school community for the benefit of future generations. Could you begin a recycling program for a material that is used abundantly? Could you beautify a wall, a hall, a classroom with recycled materials? In Durham, North Carolina, a business called the Scrap Exchange provides excess foam, textiles, and myriad plastic products to use for playful constructions, such as costumes and decorations. Invite students to bring in and use such materials.

> *By looking closely at the natural world, we may learn*
> *anew what the deepest spiritual traditions of humanity*
> *have always taught; namely, that there is an ultimate*
> *and sacred unity.*
>
> —Rick Fields

Reflection

How do I appreciate my interconnectedness with the earth?

What's Your Favorite Color?

Awareness ~

How can I deepen students' understanding of color?

Color can be stimulating or depressing, constructive or destructive. It can be repellent or attractive. Each color has its own unique effects and can be used for healing and balancing, as well as for stimulating deeper levels of consciousness.

—Ted Andrews

We all have strong feelings regarding color. With ease we identify colors we adore and those we hate. A colleague once demanded of me, "How could you possibly have a red car? I just don't like that color!" I looked at her bright green car and shot back, "How could you have such a bright green car? It looks like an Easter egg!" We both laughed and, ever the art teachers, shrugged and noted that, "Well, at least they're complementary colors!" One day I sat behind a forest green sports-utility vehicle at a traffic light, trying to decode the vanity tag. Then I finally got it, linking the color of the car to the license, which read: "W/ ENVY."

CULTURAL PHILOSOPHIES

Color is an integral part of everyday life; we are drawn to certain hues for our furniture, our clothing, and our smallest of personal possessions. Color tinges the language we use to describe our feelings, such as "I'm so angry I see red," "I have the blues," or "It was a golden moment." Fast food franchises know that yellow stimulates the appetite; athletic teams have been wise enough to provide soothing, mellow blue walls for the visiting team's locker room but reserve the fiery, adrenaline-pumping orange walls in the locker room for their home-game pep talks.

The human eye can see approximately 30 to 40 values of one color alone. Sir Isaac Newton's discovery of the spectrum of pure colors led him to chart the colors in what we now know as the color wheel. In the branch of science known as photobiology, scientists study the effects of light and color, both visible and invisible, on humans and other living organisms. Medical science uses light therapy for some types of depression, and branches of alternative medicine use color to heal certain ailments. Psychologist Carl Jung thought of light as a metaphor for enlightenment and mystical experiences. While in Western science the rainbow is white light being refracted through a prism into individual colors, Tibetan yogis call a *rainbow body* the subtle body of an enlightened yogi. In the Bible's story of Genesis, the rainbow symbolizes God's covenant and spiritual protection. Each of the seven chakras of the Hindu tradition relates to one of the colors of the rainbow as well as a specific sound. Certain Native Americans, such as the Zuni, Cherokee, and Chippewa, have various colors assigned to the four directions, with each tribe selecting different colors. The Plains Indians associate white with the north, relating it to wisdom, while in the Tantric yoga tradition, white is the color of water, representing anger, clarity, and the East.

LESSON IDEAS

1. Have students research their favorite color. They can look at the historical and scientific meanings behind certain colors, such as the fact that purple has traditionally been a color reserved for royalty because purple dyes were once so expensive. Here are some questions to guide their work:

- What symbolic meanings, healing properties, or emotional connections are associated with certain colors? How are these similar and different among cultures?
- Where and when does your favorite color appear in the natural world around you?
- Where is your favorite color reflected in your personal environment?

2. In the spirit of abstract expressionists, have students create a collage using only the color they have chosen. Color-field painters such as Josef Albers, Clyfford Still, and Mark Rothko made their mark within the American movement of abstract expressionism by concentrating on the expressive qualities of color. Instead of drawing detailed figures or contrasting lights and darks, they covered huge canvases with one solid color or a color with a small range of values, affecting the viewer with a huge, infinite-seeming blast of emotional brilliance. Using magazines or colored scraps of paper, students can cut color swatches and place them creatively on a blank sheet of white paper. Encourage students to create ranges of color, such as a progression of light to dark values. Compositions can be abstract (like a cubist Picasso) or nonobjective (having no defined objects present, like a Jackson Pollock).

3. After creating a color collage, students can complete a short writing assignment on their chosen color. Some may want to write a paragraph in passionate defense of this color and why it outshines the rest; others may want to discuss the relative merits of certain colors. Students can present their projects as mini oral reports. These writings can then be framed by the artistic renderings for a powerful display.

They came to a place where they could see from above a line of light, straight as a column, extending right through the whole heaven and through the earth, in color resembling the rainbow, only brighter and purer . . . and there, in the midst of the light, they saw the ends of the chains of heaven let down from above: for this light is the belt of heaven, and holds together the circle of the universe.

—Plato

Reflection

What is my understanding of color?

LESSON 3
Don't You Want to Know?

Curiosity ~⌒~

How do I cultivate my students' spirit of curiosity?

Questions are the creative acts of intelligence.
—Frank Kingdon

"Why do you think it is," a colleague asked me one day, "that our students are so grade-focused?" Tired and preoccupied, I swiftly provided the pat answer of a frustrated teacher. "It's the home life," I said. "If the parents value learning rather than striving after material things, then you see that ethic in the kids." We then commiserated over the frequent questions of "What's my grade?" and "How long does this have to be?" I was in the mood to complain, not solve the problem; I was not curious about how to address this issue. Perhaps there was some truth to my remark, but when I thought more deeply about the issue, I acknowledged that a teacher's calling is not to polish bars of gold that appear on the classroom doorstep. Instead the vocation is to refine whatever might arrive, and all too often, students arrive without much curiosity.

CULTURAL PHILOSOPHIES

Students may not realize—and we as teachers may have forgotten—that questions form the root of every discipline. Many of the world's great spiritual teachers were once students who dared to seek answers to the tough questions. Zen Buddhism is famous for its mind-boggling stories and verses that inspire their listeners to delve deeply into the nature of self, one's relationship with the earth, and the nature of life. These challenges are often in the form of straight questions or metaphorical folk stories, such as a dialogue between a Zen master and his disciple. A teacher will hand a disciple a *koan* (a paradox), and the student may solve it immediately or take years to ponder it. When a student meditates on the central point of the exchange—a question or statement—rational structure and traditional habits of reviewing problems collapse. Thus koans inspire mystical insight, a transcendent way of seeing the world, because one's curiosity leads to seeking answers with a relentless fervor, and truth is revealed. Perhaps you have already heard:

- What is the sound of one hand clapping?
- When you can do nothing, what can you do?
- What is the color of wind?

In his book *Conceptual Blockbusting*, Jim Adams (2001) notes that "most of the questions you used to wonder about in your youth (What is beyond the farthest star? What is life? Why do people die?) are still unanswered" (106). Author and consultant Rachael Kessler suggests in *The Soul of Education* (2000) that life's most pressing and unanswerable questions, those queries that most fascinate adolescents, become the center of our curriculum.

LESSON IDEAS

1. Pose thematic questions to frame your units of study so that students are constantly engaged in problem solving. See authors Grant Wiggins and Jay McTighe (1998) for ideas.

2. Encourage your students to consider presenting oral reports on topics they have always been curious about or areas in which they strive for expertise. I have had students present on the art of low-

rider bicycle maintenance, fishing, and yoga—talents and skills about which students have no end of curiosity. This project is a great self-esteem builder for all students. At one school, I arranged a week of mini-courses and workshops where students who wished to teach could showcase their skills and students who wished to learn more about the topic could attend.

> *The wisdom of the novel comes from having a question for everything.*
> —Milan Kundera

Reflection

How do I cultivate my own curiosity?

LESSON 4
What Did You Say?

Connotation

How can I help students celebrate the power of words?

> *In the beginning was the Word, and the Word was with God, and the Word was God.*
>
> —John 1:1

In all my years of schooling, one of the more memorable statements I heard from a teacher is a commentary on a single word. Within a few seconds, my eighth-grade teacher made me think seriously about the power of the word "hate." " 'Hate' is such a strong word," she said. "It's not to be used casually, as in 'I hate spaghetti.' Remember to use it sparingly, if at all." I took her advice to heart. I find today that I still restrain myself if that utterance comes to mind; I sense that once expressed, such a word can act powerfully in the world to cause harm. Today as a teacher, I persist in encouraging students to choose their words carefully. When callous expressions in vogue, such as "That sucks" or "That's retarded,'" burst out in class, I ask students to speak more delicately and kindly. And I delight in those rare but wonderful moments when a student shares her rapture with the power of beautiful language. One day a student approached me at the end of class, after I had assigned the last pages of Shakespeare's *The Tempest*. "Oh, the ending," she gasped, referring to the epilogue. "Oh, it was so beautiful. I had tears in my eyes." I was moved just hearing her speak. Her delight

91

and passion for the play transported me back to my first reading of Macbeth's tragic soliloquy:

> *Tomorrow, and tomorrow, and tomorrow*
> *Creeps in this petty pace from day to day* (V, v, 19–20)

That text begged to be spoken, not only because it is part of a script, but also because the language sings when you say it. One can only marvel at the incandescence of the mind, as Virginia Woolf once noted, that could craft such lines. The droning repetition of certain words, the clipped alliteration, and the compelling imagery all weave together to portray the loneliest of men, mired in ennui. As a teen who found solace in reading and reflection, I thrilled to the sound of words more than three hundred years old that spoke to my own alienation as well as my sense of beauty. Today the language is no less powerful: It demands my full attention, my time to absorb it, and always my voice.

CULTURAL PHILOSOPHIES

Words possess incredible connotative power. A word can spark a wealth of associations, resonating for each person quite differently in a multitude of directions. Words produce thousands of pictures for those who are willing to play with them. All language is, in fact, metaphor: a visual snapshot of meaning that alludes to the depth of the word but never quite the whole of it. West African, Vedic, and Judeo-Christian spiritual traditions have acknowledged the power of the sacred Word to create the universe. The Fon People of Benin (Nigeria) tell a creation story that starts with God vocalizing his will through the word, known as *Fa,* of Mawu-Lisa. Sanskrit scriptures describe the sustained, methodical practice of mantra meditation, a process handed down from teacher to disciple. Early Christians who sought the desert in the first millennium also practiced mantra meditation, and now this tradition has been revived among Christians. "The Word" itself is a powerful symbol to Christians, derived from the Greek *logos,* which means not only word but also the reason or principle behind the entire universe. These Western and Eastern faiths have found the mantra to be a sacred expression of the Absolute Truth, or God. A mantra, a mystical invocation of particular words to which the speaker or faith attaches a power, is in actuality beyond words. By saying a mantra, the speaker hopes to connect with spirit. According to Vedic tradition, the core of a mantra is unadulterated, uncreated, infinite sound, known as *nada*. Nada speaks to the creative source behind all mantras, unknown and yet knowable through a metaphorical word chosen by humans striving to find the true essence of God.

LESSON IDEAS

1. Find a short text that you and your students can savor. Ask students to work in pairs to read aloud to each another and concentrate on particular words that strike them as important or beautifully written. After reading the text aloud two or three times, each student should tell her partner her personal translation of the passage. As you wander about the classroom, listen for important clues about your students' reading comprehension and for evidence of your students' gifts for speaking and performing. Then ask the class to share aloud any golden lines they have read.

2. Model for students how to savor a text. Read a selection of humor, irony, or any other human-interest text connected to your subject area. As you read aloud, indicate your pleasure when hearing an elegant or powerful line. In that powerful moment of silence following a reading, let words settle in the bones and drift into the soul.

3. Celebrate the power of language by asking students to play with words. Ask students to make lists of favorite words that refer to people, objects, actions, emotions, experiences, and dreams that they value. Encourage students to brainstorm nouns, verbs, adjectives, and adverbs so that they create a rich variety of options for the poetry activity.

4. When students arrive the next day, ask them to think about where they want to be and what they want to be doing five, ten, and fifteen years from now. Tell them to write down 10 meaningful words that relate to their goals and aspirations for their lives, each on a separate slip of paper. For example, a student might write *fly, degree, love, dynamic, thoughtfully, challenge, hope, romance, adventurous, bravely*. Then ask each student to pick his five favorite words.

5. Have students work in pairs or triads to compose a poem that celebrates the versatility and magic of their favorite words. Tell students that their goal is to see their words in new ways and play with language. Each student may bring only five words to this

exercise. The group may add a few pronouns, articles, or prepositions where necessary. Once these poems are complete, have students share them with the class.

> For an extension of this activity, ask students to create a private poem of favorite words and to identify one or two "power words," those that make them happy when they think of them. Students can decorate personal possessions with these words.

6. Ask these groups of two or three to migrate to become a group of four, five, or six with another group of students. Now the group has five words multiplied by the number of people in the group for use in writing a new poem.

7. Ask groups to read their poetry aloud. In between the nonsense lines, some gems will emerge. Dialogue with students:

   • How did your word's meaning transform when it joined other words?

   • What golden lines emerge from the combination of words?

The thought manifests as the word,
The word manifests as the deed,
The deed develops into habit,
And the habit hardens into character
So watch the thought
And its ways with care,
And let it spring from love
Born out of respect for all beings

                                    —Buddhist philosophy

Reflection

What words resonate with me?

LESSON 5

Respect
the Earth

Stewardship

How can I encourage my students to be better stewards of the earth?

> *How I long to see among dawn
> flowers, the face of God.*
>
> —Basho

On my first visit to a small college in North Carolina, I was immediately taken by the sight of two flags fluttering from the flagpole: the United States flag and a flag of Planet Earth. Like the view the astronauts must have had of the Earth, the beautiful planet of ours floated in a blue wash of sky-space on this flag. It was a reminder to me of the interconnectedness of all people as we inhabit this earth together. The smallness of the planet from space puts into perspective my sense of dual identity, that of a citizen of the United States and that of citizen of the planet. The view also reminds me that I am such a small part, yet integral to the whole.

CULTURAL PHILOSOPHIES

Planet Earth is magnificent yet fragile. Daily we move about our environment with little awareness of the complexity of the ecosystems that maintain a delicate balance here on earth. But developments of the late 20th century have led us to more awareness. We owe our thanks to many activists for changing our attitudes. In 1969, U.S. Senator Gaylord Nelson initiated Earth Day after six years of looking for a way to draw attention to the state of the environment. He was well aware that the environment was a nonissue in politics. While reading an article on teach-ins, widely held at that time to protest the Vietnam War, a wonderful idea came to him: Hold a nationwide teach-in on the planet's health. He raised funds and sent letters to all 50 governors and to mayors of all the major cities, an article to all college newspapers, and one letter to *Scholastic* magazine to target grade and high schools. He requested that an Earth Day Proclamation be enacted. The story hit the presses nationwide; calls and letters from across the United States swamped his office. Even with the help of his Senate staff, he still required more space, and so he opened an office in Washington to serve as the National Clearinghouse for Earth Day. By the spring of 1970, he had achieved his goal of bringing national attention and political awareness to environmental concerns, as an estimated 20 million people participated in activities across the nation on April 22. Included in that figure were 10,000 grade schools and high schools, 2,000 colleges, and 1,000 communities. His original Earth Day office closed immediately following the event, but the celebration has continued. On the 20th anniversary, more than 200 million people in 141 countries celebrated Earth Day, proving the power of grass-roots activism. Earth Day USA now has permanent offices with staff fielding questions, fundraising, and creating data sheets and activities.

LESSON IDEAS

1. Initiate an Earth Day celebration at your school. Ask teachers who are interested to devote their classes that day to topics that relate to the earth in their respective disciplines. The opportunities for teaching about the wonders of the earth are endless. Some successful activities include making soap from natural ingredients in

science class; estimating the amount of trash generated daily by the school in math class; making recycled paper and reading and writing nature poems in English class; making nature prints in art class; and discussing environmental movements and degradation of resources in various countries in foreign-language and social studies classes.

> *Sympathy with nature is part of the good man's religion.*
> —F. H. Hedge

2. Project ideas beyond the classroom could include beginning a garden or forming a partnership with an area botanical garden to identify plants in an area yet unexplored near campus.

3. Local communities often sponsor Earth Day celebrations, and you can encourage students to meet at one of these events. My students and I have attended the Earth Day celebration in our area and delighted in booths such as the Scrap Exchange, which allowed us to help local children make art from scrap. Multicolored jester hats made out of cardboard cones and old stockings, purses made with plastic netting, and giant dragonflies made from foam scraps delighted young children and my older students as well. These were the best kind of toys: community-made and recycled.

Reflection

How can I show greater stewardship for the earth?

LESSON 6
What a Coincidence

Meaning ～～～

How can I help my students reflect on the meaning of their lives?

> *We are not in this life merely by accident, playing out a meaningless drama. Our lives have purpose, a sense of destiny. We seem to be guided forward by a mysterious providence.*
>
> —James Redfield

More than once in my early years of teaching I would become depressed and worried about a particular student's fate. This student would be going downhill fast, making what seemed to be the worst choices possible. At one of these times, my teaching mentor caught me in a low moment and heard the story with my sad tag line: "She doesn't respond to anyone's help." My mentor offered this wisdom: "In a child's life, there may be 20 souls who reach out to him. You don't know if you are number 3 or number 13 to intervene, but all these efforts can weave together until something clicks for the child and he is ready to respond." When I thought about what she had said, I realized that my and others' seemingly random and ineffective attempts to help a person were actually forming an uplifting pattern of "lucky breaks" or "guardian angels." Fate could be better known as providence: uncanny, perhaps supernatural guidance and care to aid a struggling soul. My overtures to the student were a meaningful link in the chain of providence.

CULTURAL PHILOSOPHIES

What series of unforeseen and sometimes inexplicable events led you into the teaching profession? Is there an invisible sequence of well-timed choices and chances leading to this very moment? For many around the world, spiritual beliefs illuminate and interpret connections that seem to emerge among these life events. To keep on living day to day, some trust in the seeming plan before them—that they are meant to live at least another day, year, or forever to accomplish a unique destiny. The human insistence on finding ways to link what others might deem meaningless moments is universal: People seek out patterns with the tenacity of scientists, discovering order in the chaos. In his book *West African Traditional Religion,* Kofi Asare Opoku (1978) shares how the Akan and the Gonja peoples of Ghana have the following beliefs about God's providence, respectively: that it is unfailing—"If God gives you a cup of wine and an evil-minded person kicks it over, He fills it up for you again"—and that it is timely —"God arranges things so that a leper's sandal breaks under the camel foot shrub, which provides the rope to mend it" (28). Meaning might be found by those who read the Christian author St. Paul, who writes that "in all things God works for the good of those who love him, who have been called according to his purpose" (Romans 8:28, New International version). In Islam, this concept that everything is emerging from God, being sustained by God, and returning to God is known as *tawid.* God is the Oneness that is basis for all existence. Rabbi Joseph Telushkin (1994) speaks in *Jewish Wisdom* of a late 19th-century Hasidic rabbi who told his followers, "Everything that has been created in God's world has a lesson to teach us." Thinking the rabbi was speaking in hyperbole, one of the listeners called out, "And what can we learn from the telegraph?" "That for every word you pay," replied the rabbi. "And what from the telephone?" asked another. "That what we say here," he answered, "is heard there" (45).

LESSON IDEAS

1. Tell your students that they will be reflecting on patterns and meaning among events in their lives. Ask them to define "coincidence." Webster tells us that a coincidence is "the occurrence of events that happen at the same time by accident but seem to have some connection." Today they will be reflecting on this connection.

2. Ask students to think about a passion—a talent or interest that they have—and write about that passion in a journal entry. They might think about the following questions:

   - What is your passion?
   - Why do you pursue it now?
   - Which circumstances led to it? (For example, a child who loves basketball might remember Grandpa teaching her to play hoops at age four, and then the basketball games on TV that inspired her to play ball with a local league, and then the coach who let her try to play center one day. These events all worked together to make her the basketball player that she is today.)
   - Which circumstances seem like coincidences? Which seem like choices?
   - Do you believe that this passion was meant to be? Why?
   - In what ways has this passion made a difference in your life?
   - What lessons and insights emerge for you because of this passion?

3. Ask students to think of a symbol that is representative of the life events that led to this passion. Have each student then create a chain of events in the likeness of a string of old-fashioned paper dolls. They should fold a piece of paper like an accordion and then draw the symbol on the top of the folded paper. They should also draw tabs to the folded edges so that the symbols stay attached. Then they cut the image out to produce a string of repeated images. When I demonstrated this activity to my high school students, I used an apple as a symbol of my passion for teaching.

4. Have the students make a list of key words representing different life events that built this passion. The basketball player might choose a ball as a symbol and on the first one write "Grandpa," on

the second, "WNBA games," and on the third, "Coach Phillips, center." These words should trigger stories of special meaning for the individual.

> *God does not play dice with the universe.*
> —Albert Einstein

5. When their symbol chains and journal entries are finished, invite students to mingle in small groups and share the stories behind the symbols. When the whole class reconvenes, invite each group to encourage a certain individual to share his stories.

6. A follow-up activity could be for students to discuss or write another journal entry on these questions: Which events in your life seem most providential? Which events are you most grateful for and why? They could also write notes or letters of gratitude to those who helped make their passion possible.

Reflection

What meaning do I find among the events in my life?

LESSON 7

Go Ahead and Cry

Grief

How can I help my students experience grief?

If we could see that everything, even tragedy,
is a gift in disguise, we would then find the
best way to nourish the soul.

—Elisabeth Kübler-Ross

Catherine was a junior at our school who knew that we all needed to confront the Columbine tragedy. She was particularly touched by the event because she had once lived close to Littleton, Colorado. She took it upon herself to organize a memorial service soon after the incident. The day we had the assembly, a few students griped that there was no point to this ceremony. They seemed hardened to the tragedy, viewing it as simply one of many other news events. But many members of our school community were touched by the experience of an emotional ritual. Students read poetry, fastened blue ribbons to their shirts, listened to a S.A.V.E. (Students Against Violence Everywhere) speaker, and sat in silent meditation on the lost lives. Even if Catherine herself had been the only one moved by the experience, she ensured that we all paused and acknowledged the wrong that had occurred. Many of us realized that we were not powerless: We could actively grieve.

CULTURAL PHILOSOPHIES

Earthquakes. Hurricanes. The terrorist attacks of September 11, 2001. We are often overwhelmed by the successions of tragedies across the globe that visit us through the news. Added to these traumas are the personal trials that each of us must endure, including deaths in the family, divorces, and disease. When we grieve, many layers of our being experience the pain. We employ our rationality to understand why a tragedy has occurred; we create ritual to commemorate our loss and provide an outlet for our emotions; we seek spiritual sustenance as we integrate the loss into our lives. Often we must witness our students learning that grief is a normal and inevitable part of their lives. We can help them understand that it is healthy to spend time grieving. In her book *The New American Spirituality,* Elizabeth Lesser (1999) writes, "To grieve well the passing away of anyone or anything—a parent, a love, a child, an era, a home, a job—is a spiritual skill worth developing. It helps us make sense of our lives; it reveals to us our deeper feelings; and it encourages us to let go and move on. Instead of freezing up inside and pretending that loss doesn't touch us close to the bone, or instead of squandering our energy, holding tight against the flow of life, full-bodied grieving acts like a tonic. It purifies and revivifies" (296).

LESSON IDEAS

1. When a tragedy strikes, teachers are on the front lines to help students understand the event. We are responsible for modeling a healthy and compassionate approach to pain. Provide students with time to ask questions, comment, write, or create art about a tragic event. These opportunities can be class activities or homework. Sometimes suspending regular homework to allow students to process an event through a journal entry or an art project completed at home might be more effective than trying to lead a discussion with a whole group at school. Every class chemistry and each individual is different, and sometimes the seeming apathy of one group or student can disguise profound emotions that students are experiencing but unable to share with others.

2. Provide a safe space for conversation or silence when needed. Sometimes, it is important to stop class to allow students to vent, question, or even be silent. Psychologist and school consultant

Robert Evans (2001) offers this advice for handling difficult questions: "Often a request for information is spurred not only by curiosity, but by a feeling . . . We may be more helpful if, rather than plunging into an immediate answer, we learn what motivates the question . . . 'What made you think of that?' or 'Can you tell me what you were thinking about?' Also, it can be good to ask 'What ideas do you have?' Once you know the meaning of the question, it is easier to answer effectively . . . There may be questions we cannot answer, which can make us feel inadequate. But children and teenagers are typically more comforted by straight talk than by false assurances. Rather than to invent a response, it can be much more helpful to say, 'I don't know,' or, 'I'll try to find out' (1–2).

3. Sometimes a simple addition to the classroom can make a difference, to let students know that the events that inspired grief are not forgotten. Posting inspirational quotations or messages of comfort each week can be of help.

4. In the case of a local or national tragedy, work together with colleagues to answer tough questions, such as "How much—if any—TV should we watch?" "What do my students most need to know now?" or, "What kinds of discussions should we have, and what kinds of activities might be helpful?" Inform students of the information that is most important for them to have so that fears can be allayed and classes can proceed. If your school has not informed you of its plan for crisis management, inquire as to what it is so that you can be better prepared.

5. In all cases of an individual student's loss, seek guidance from school counselors to ensure that involving students or the community is acceptable with the family. While some families and students welcome community support, others may lead private lives and prefer to contain their grief among family members. Community support may include a group card or a welcoming embrace when the student comes back to school.

6. Let students know you are grieving, too, if applicable. You can share your confusion and pain and questions by briefly mentioning that you also struggle and need time to process what is happening.

I share with my students how my journal is a place for me to process pain and emotions, and I provide students opportunities to do the same in their journals.

7. Decide what you can do as a class or a school to help. Fundraisers, projects, and teach-ins are excellent options. See if students wish to create a community art project, such as a mural or garden, to respond to tragedy. Some projects have included quilts made by students or concerned citizens that, once created, circulate within the community. One well-known project is the AIDS quilt that has traveled to various sites in the world. See Happy Holidays!, on page 46, for a prayer quilt activity. Support and guide student ideas as best you can by scheduling specific times for activities to occur, coordinating necessary materials, and delegating responsibilities. Perhaps a simple ceremony in your school auditorium can bring your community together to share in a moment of silence and send a blessing to those in need.

> *There is a sacredness in tears. They are not the mark of weakness, but of power. They speak more eloquently than ten thousand tongues. They are the messengers of overwhelming grief, of deep contrition, and of unspeakable love.*
> —Washington Irving

Reflection

How do I give myself time, space, and permission to grieve?

Let Go of That

Sacrifice

How can I help my students understand the importance of sacrifice?

Eliminate something superfluous from your life. Break a habit. Do something that makes you feel insecure. Carry out an action with complete attention and intensity, as if it were your last.

—Piero Ferrucci

When I was a child, my elementary school celebrated Lent with a particular tradition: a box in the hallway full of suggestions. Each day, we were expected to reach inside and pick one. This slip of paper would instruct us in our daily sacrifice for the season. Today I might give up chocolate; tomorrow I might erase the board for the teacher; the next day I might pray for someone. These pieces of paper were small challenges to think beyond myself about others' needs and to discipline myself to do without the typical self-absorption. Symbolic acts and images, such as the almsgiving of the Lenten box, praying and fasting, and ashes on the forehead in the sign of the cross, are

Christian traditions representing sorrow for sin and the hope of resurrection during the Easter season. Many years later, as a teacher, my eyes would also be opened to learn that other faiths had symbolic acts of sacrifice to teach values and to reflect on humanity.

CULTURAL PHILOSOPHIES

In Islam, Ramadan is a season of purification, self-denial, and almsgiving. During this time, Muslim students manage an entire day of school without food and do it willingly. Muslims believe the experience of letting go of what once seemed so essential cultivates several virtues: a deep love for something transcendent, a sound conscience that is committed to fasting, a continuing patience and willpower during deprivation of food and liquid, and a spirit of community. The spirit of thankfulness to Allah and seeking forgiveness of past sins pervades this holiday. After a day that might include not only a regular work schedule but also hours of praying and studying the Qur'an, families come together in evening gatherings when the fast is broken each night. People pray, *Allah humma laka sumna, wa 'ala rizqika aftarna* (O God! For Your sake have we fasted and now we break the fast with the food You have given us). Ramadan ends with Id-al-Fitr, the Feast of Fast Breaking. A national holiday in most Muslim countries, it is celebrated with socializing, eating, and gifts for the children. Though abstinence from food and drink 12 hours a day for an entire month may seem like a hardship, many Muslims say that they find the season uplifting. They feel strengthened, disciplined, and purified by the experience.

The messages of other spiritual traditions also teach that a grasping spirit is a selfish spirit. The addictive pursuit of food and drink, drugs and alcohol, material goods and amusements can imprison a person. Just as the Qur'an speaks to human reason, encouraging that people keep their rationality unfettered by appetites and lusts, so does the Hebrew book the Talmud warn: "The more flesh, the more worms. The more possessions, the more worry." Many religions provide opportunities to abstain from certain physical pleasures and to reflect on what is important in life. Faiths such as Buddhism, Hinduism, Jainism, and several Native American spiritual beliefs employ fasting to achieve communion with the divine. In Taiwan, the Daoists celebrate a ceremony called the Jiao. In this celebration, Daoist priests act on behalf of the community to renew their connection with a trinity of primeval Daoist beings, known as the Three Pure Ones. The whole community prepares by fasting, and the ritual itself is witnessed only by priests and benefactors of the temple.

Spiritual practices also encourage a person to look outward toward the needs of others. In Judaism, contribution, or tzedakah, boxes in homes and synagogues are ways for people to express charity through community outreach and service to others. Little sacrifices such as fasting are paradoxically a kind of sustenance: When we sacrifice, our spirit is nourished. Resisting temptation also assists others in myriad ways. Giving something, especially when it is unsolicited, can surprise another to the point of changing his behavior.

LESSON IDEAS

1. Ask students to think about a time when they sacrificed something and how that affected their character. Tell a story of a sacrifice you have made and how despite difficulty it made you a better person.

2. Brainstorm the little gifts of sacrifice that we can make in our daily interactions, using the categories found in Mohammed's quotation on page 109 to help students think of ideas. List students' ideas on the board. Here are some suggestions:

   - Giving up a habit that is unhealthy or selfish
   - Not complaining when you don't have "first dibs" on something
   - Being kind or patient with someone who irritates you
   - Picking up after yourself when you're tempted to let someone else take care of it
   - Picking up litter that is not yours
   - Speaking out against gossip though you are afraid of being mocked for doing so
   - Slowing down to hold the door for another person, instead of letting it slam
   - Sharing a treat or giving it away
   - Thinking of ways to say thank you and gifts to give, instead of thinking of things you want

3. After covering the board with ideas, ask students to put their favorites on small slips of paper and fold them up. Place all of these in a small box. Invite students at the beginning of a class period to select a slip, read its message, and try to follow its suggestion during the day.

> *Every good act is charity. Your smiling in your brother's face, is charity; an exhortation of your fellow-man to virtuous deeds, is equal to alms-giving; your putting a wanderer in the right road, is charity; your assisting the blind, is charity; your removing stones, and thorns, and other obstructions from the road, is charity; your giving water to the thirsty, is charity. A man's true wealth hereafter, is the good he does in this world to his fellow-man. When he dies, people will say, 'What property has he left behind him?' But the angels will ask, 'What good deeds has he sent before him?'*
>
> —Mohammed

Reflection

What am I willing to let go?

Let's Look at a Map

Empathy

How can I evoke empathy for other cultures in my students?

> *Every moment of our life is relationship.*
> *There is nothing except relationship.*
>
> —Charlotte Joko Beck

My class of ninth graders held its breath. James, a boy with mild cerebral palsy, was attempting to read aloud, and his voice fought to express itself. We listened in awkward silence. This time he was not reading a dispassionate section of text but a personal essay. It was his story of struggle, a tale that reached far beyond his physical limitations. He and his family had escaped their war-torn homeland and had lived on a boat with hardly any food and water for many days. We watched his lips make a concentrated effort to pronounce words; tears welled up in our eyes as we began to understand the breadth of hardship that he as well as others from his country had experienced. Our classroom was so much richer for knowing James's story. We had been privileged to see through his eyes another land, a historical period, an individual soul.

CULTURAL PHILOSOPHIES

Educators Grant Wiggins and Jay McTighe (1998) discuss the importance of building and assessing our students' level of empathy in their curriculum design book *Understanding by Design*. They write that empathy is "the ability to walk in another's shoes . . . a learned ability to grasp the world from someone else's point of view. It is the discipline of using one's imagination to see and feel as others see and feel. . . . [It] suggests not merely an intellectual change of mind but a significant change of heart. Empathy requires respect for people different from ourselves" (56–57). This is the center of being humane human beings—actively showing openness to others, especially those strangers who are different from all that we know. Now that the global community is becoming increasingly accessible through travel, the Internet, and other media, teachers may use these resources to inspire an excitement, curiosity, and respect for other ways and other peoples. Exploring other cultures is one way that the teacher can help to promote understanding, appreciation, and peace. Questions focusing student research can reflect the desire of the Lakota prayer: "Great Spirit, help me never to judge another until I have walked two weeks in his moccasins."

LESSON IDEAS

1. Gather around a world map with your students. Invite them to point to the names of places around the world they would like to visit or have visited. Ask each student to choose one place or cultural group that he already knows from that region.

> This activity can be easily adapted to any course. A math teacher, for example, might adapt the questions to center on famous mathematicians in a specific culture or region of the world, or a science teacher could illustrate the achievements of scientists from around the globe. History teachers could lead students to research Nobel Prize winners for peace, science, math, and literature.

2. Ask students to investigate media resources to make discoveries about the cultures they chose. Explain to students that their goal is to learn as much as they can in order to get inside another person's feelings and worldview. Here are questions to help students focus their research:

> Several great resources, such as *Faces* magazine, *New Moon,* and *Teaching Tolerance,* can provide inspirational articles and visuals. World literature provides many opportunities for further investigation of cultures. If possible, show the short video *It's in Every One of Us* (Krutein and Pomeranz 1987) before students begin their work. It is a "world tour" of faces that will bring tears to your eyes. For more in-depth studies, try *African Journey* (Bloomfield 1989), an excellent Wonderworks family movie that shows how a Canadian boy and an African boy build a friendship.

- What is a unique custom that this cultural group practices? What is the meaning behind the custom? What can you appreciate about this custom? What customs does your culture or heritage share with this culture?

- What greetings do people exchange in this culture—words and gestures? What are their meanings and origin? How do you feel as you practice or explore this style of greeting?

- What is an art form of this culture? What is expressed though this art form? How is art integrated into daily life? How is beauty defined in this culture? What symbols or ritual observances are reflected in artmaking?

- How is food prepared and served in this culture? What are key ingredients? Why are certain tastes and food groups valued? If ingredients are foreign to you, how can you investigate them? Are there cultural or religious ceremonies or rituals around eating, preparing, planting, or harvesting food?

- What are some of the spiritual beliefs held by these people? How would you describe their worldview? How does this view remind you of philosophies you have encountered before? At what point do you struggle to understand the belief? Why?

- What is the experience of youths your age in this country? What in their experience sounds familiar? What must you try to understand?

- What barriers do you see between our culture and this other culture you have studied? What stereotypes exist, and how are they harmful? What are ways you would suggest to eliminate such barriers and stereotypes? How can these new ideas be integrated into your daily life?

- What are creative ways in which you can express the wisdom you have gained from this study?

- What can you share with your classmates about your own heritage to help others understand a new culture or tradition?

> *The divine beauty of heaven and earth,*
> *All creation, members of one family.*
> —Morihei Ueshiba

Reflection

How can I develop greater empathy for other cultures?

LESSON 10
Smile!

Joy

How can I encourage my students to smile today?

Your mindful breath and your smile will bring happiness to you and those around you. Even if you spend a lot of money on gifts for everyone . . . nothing you could buy them can give as much true happiness as your gift of awareness, breathing, and smiling, and these precious gifts cost nothing.

—Thich Nhat Hanh

A student in fear of failure came to my classroom one day, stressed about his grade. We talked the issue through, and at the end I looked at him and said, "Now smile for me, please!" It took a bit more prompting, but finally he was able to smile. The next day when he came back in my room, he said, "Thanks—you helped a lot!" For many years I have made a point to stand outside the classroom and greet students with a smile, looking into their eyes and letting them know I am glad to see them. Many times these students have come from difficult situations, but often these are the students who hand out high-fives, big hugs, and beaming smiles in return. In some cases, I knew intuitively that my greeting was the highlight of their day. A colleague of another race once told me that I was "different" from others of my racial background because I smiled at everyone. Though I told him I was just doing what came naturally, he asserted that my friendliness helped cross the boundaries of racial polarization at our school. He reminded me that the simplicity of a smile provides countless gifts.

CULTURAL PHILOSOPHIES

Studies report that smiling can release certain endorphins within our bodies that actually create a chemical change. The action sparks a positive shift in our environment and in us. In his book *Awakening to the Sacred,* Lama Surya Das (1999) suggests a simple meditation to help us make this transition: Breathe, smile, and relax. Do it several times, and do it anywhere: in the car at a red light, in the lunchroom, at your desk, or during a lesson. When you think of moments in your life when you were preoccupied or anxious and a smile from a stranger or a friend made a moment in time so much better, you realize that practicing such an exercise as Das's is essential. You know that the world becomes a much softer, more enchanting place, simply by your smiling. When one sees a statue of the Buddha, he is always smiling, which is a reflection of inner peace and contentment. There is a discipline to cultivating joy that does not come naturally in a world weighed down with worry and complications. The old educator's adage, "Don't smile till December," has calcified the faces of too many new teachers who are afraid of losing classroom control. But with time teachers begin to know the appropriate moments to smile and the times to be serious. A teacher may choose not to smile while enforcing discipline or establishing expectations. But beyond the tough-love times, the opportunities for grinning are endless. Smiling may seem like a simple act that does not require special attention, but when it touches a person's day with kindness, the effects can be profound.

LESSON IDEAS

1. Breathe, smile, relax. Lead students in this meditation.

2. Consider meeting your students at the door each morning, to smile, shake hands, and break the ice before the business of class gets rolling.

3. Remind yourself throughout the day to breathe, smile, and relax.

> *The fullness of joy is to behold God in everything.*
> —Mother Julian of Norwich,
>   14th-century mystic

Reflection

When do I find myself smiling in my classroom?

Summer

Rest is not idleness, and to lie sometimes on the grass on a summer day listening to the murmur of water, or watching the clouds float across the sky, is hardly a waste of time.

—John Lubbock

LESSON 1

Don't You See?

Seeing

How can I encourage my students to see the natural world with awe and appreciation?

In this twentieth century, to stop rushing around, to sit quietly on the grass, to switch off the world and come back to the earth, to allow the eye to see a willow, a bush, a cloud, a leaf, is 'an unforgettable experience.'

—Frederick Franck

One of my past classrooms looked out on a wooded area full of pine trees. Every once in a while I would pause and become aware of their beauty. I was reminded of the great American painters who like Grant Wood captured the beauty of a haystack or like Albert Bierstadt rendered the majestic vistas of Yosemite. I thought about painter Georgia O'Keeffe, who would take an object from nature such as a flower and draw and magnify it numerous times, rendering the object unrecognizable as she gloried in its shape, shadow, and color. Through the simplicity of lines, she expressed timeless beauty and elegance. As I gazed out my window, I realized how few times during a day I thought of the earth and all its splendor. My daily routine took place within the confines of human-made walls. Before I knew it, I would be heading home, lamenting the fact that I had had no experiences out-of-doors. But one of my colleagues actively fought this "stay inside" mentality. She would ask her young students to go outside in pairs, with one in each pair blindfolded. Instructed to be a guide who moved slowly and safely, the other student would lead his partner to something of beauty. Once this tree, flower, or bird was in view, the guide would squeeze his partner's hand. She would remove her blindfold to observe at close range whatever was in front of her. The teacher encouraged the students to approach this natural marvel as if seeing it for the first time.

CULTURAL PHILOSOPHIES

Summer is a wondrous time to see nature at its fullest. The spirit of "No hurry" adopted in warmer climates, such as in the West African nation of Ghana, makes time to experience nature, reclining to glory in her fullness. All the seeds planted in spring reveal themselves to us in a riot of peak colors, and with longer days giving us a sense of more time, we look around to see the fruits of the earth and the fruits of our labors. Spiritually, our minds can rest and find calm as nature progresses toward wholeness. As we relax, we gain greater consciousness of our relationships with other people and the elements of nature. We can remember that before we built our roads, malls, and office buildings, the earth rambled in all directions, untamed and majestic. People depended on the earth and observed by necessity the natural rhythms of the day. Some indigenous tribes would sing the sun up and call the world to consciousness, believing participation was essential to the earth continuing on its course. Many spiritual traditions have taught that by looking closely at the natural world, one will see the sacred unity of all things on earth. Writer Annie Dillard shares that "an observant Jew recites a grateful prayer at seeing landscape—mountains, hills, seas, rivers and deserts, which are, one would have thought, pretty much unavoidable sights. 'Blessed art Thou, O Lord, our God, King of the Universe, THE MAKER OF ALL CREATION" (Zaleski 2000, 101). The transcendental and romantic writers and artists of the

19th century also sought to express the connection between the human and the divine through a deep and individual kinship with nature. Certain scientists have come to accept the "Gaia hypothesis," a principle used to describe the concept that the earth is a living organism. In fact, the term "matter" derives from the Latin word *mater,* or mother. Summer warms us with the remembrance of returning to the mother that has fed us with abundant blessings so that we may pay our respects.

LESSON IDEAS

1. To help your students feel again the pulse of the earth, take time with them to witness nature up close, instead of from a distance. Ask students to observe and draw something in nature. The goal is to see, truly see, all that is contained within that one small piece of nature and to draw it in detail. Encourage them to sit with some distance between themselves and the object, being silent and observing nature in stillness. They can select a portion of the whole object, such as the center of a flower or close-up of a pinecone, bark on a tree, or small branches of shrubbery.

2. Ask them to look carefully at the matter, observing all the leaves, blossoms, attachments, lines, and patterns. They should notice how it grows. Students should draw exactly what they see, capturing all the nuances of light, shadow, and line.

3. If a student says she is done, encourage her to look further. Students should keep returning to each aspect, drawing not from memory but from sight, noting not just the individual lines but the spaces between, and the shapes, thickness, and delicacy of the patterns. Their focus should be mostly on the object rather than their paper.

4. For an extension, once the drawing is complete, students can choose to add color by working with colored pencils to add another level of seeing. After completing this assignment, one of my students commented, "Wow, I never really looked at a tree like that before," and I knew she would remember this lesson.

5. Ask students to complete a descriptive paragraph that presents in words all the details they just rendered in drawing.

6. Create an art museum where students rotate to look at each other's art while trying to match anonymous descriptive paragraphs to the artwork.

> *No one ever really sees a flower anymore.*
> —Georgia O'Keeffe

Reflection

What do I see when I look at a flower?

How Can I Help You?

Kindness

How can I encourage acts of kindness?

The greatest challenge of the day is how to bring about a revolution of the heart, a revolution which has to start with each one of us.

—Dorothy Day

Our friend Beth is an anonymous angel. A talented graphic artist, she designs small, bright cards with encouraging quotations and colorful images. "What lies behind us and what lies before us are tiny matters compared to what lies within us," reads one, a saying by Oliver Wendell Holmes. She adds: "You, my dearest soul, are a miracle." She slips these cards under the windshield wipers of strangers' cars, providing little surprises to brighten someone's day. The anonymous fairy of kindness loves to strike again and again.

I once taught a small group of students who likewise found pleasure in spreading kindness. The idea germinated one afternoon in my classroom, when I needed to find a short project for students just before spring break began. I turned to them for inspiration. One said, "How about we each make a card for someone we know?" Another piped in, "Hey, we could do it anonymously and leave it for them to find." The brainstorm soon snowballed into a bimonthly ritual of making creative

and kind gifts for others. They created collage magnets for teachers, featuring words that depicted each person's special qualities. These were left in the faculty lounge with an anonymous note. Small affirmation cards appeared on lockers, and little tokens began to pop up all over the school. It was fun to hear everyone trying to figure out who was responsible for these delightful acts of kindness. The givers enjoyed the ritual as much as the recipients. After a few classes of planning gifts of generosity, the group dubbed itself the Feel Good Club. I supported their efforts with pleasure, providing them time and supplies to practice their random acts of kindness.

CULTURAL PHILOSOPHIES

Such rituals appreciate and affirm the goodness in others. They are a breath of fresh air in school cultures where students' "learning gaps" and inadequacies sometimes receive too much attention. Cultivating the spirit of love and appreciation is as much an art and a discipline as raising test scores. Schools could take their cue from a certain culture that affirms people with a special ritual at moments when they may be the hardest to love. When a member of the Babemba ethnic group of South Africa acts irresponsibly or unjustly, all work stops. This person is asked to sit alone at the center of the village. Every member of the village makes a large circle around the offender. Then every person has a chance to speak to the accused, singing his praises. Every true statement that can be made to the offender's credit is shared for all to hear by every member of the village, no matter what her age. His virtues, his past accomplishments, and his gifts to others are detailed at length. This ritual lasts until the last affirmation is exhausted, sometimes after several days. Once the affirmations cease, the village celebrates joyously to welcome the person back into community life. Likewise in the classroom can teachers and students give attention to those qualities in others that often go unnoticed and unappreciated.

LESSON IDEAS

1. See if there is a group of students in your classroom who have the desire to make and create gifts for others. Can you nurture this desire in some way? Provide the atmosphere, direction if needed, some supplies, and let them go.

2. If your students need warming up to the task, try this affirmation exercise that ends in a celebration. Ask your students to define "affirmation." Affirmations can be thought of as decisive statements that affirm something positive as already existing. Affirmations can also be thought of as "inspiring dedications" or "appreciations." Students can brainstorm a list of original nominations for skills and gifts that make the class a community: "someone who shares well"; "someone who is not afraid to be herself"; "a person for whom I've gained a new respect."

3. Once students understand the meaning, ask them to record in an artistic form a few of these positive statements about others. Assign each student a number of names (I told my students to count off the three people to their right) and write those down. They can write and illustrate their affirmation on small scraps of colored paper, using markers or crayons.

4. Have everyone prepare for a toasting party where each person in the class is recognized with these affirmations. For the party, assign everyone a person to toast. Give class time for the toaster to read over the three affirmation cards written about a person. The toaster should then write a small speech that incorporates a fourth affirmation and finishes with the other three in the best possible order. Students can begin with lines such as, "I would like to honor (name the student) for his wonderful qualities . . ." or "Let's all raise our glasses to (name the student), who always shows us that she is . . ."

Scatter joy.
—Ralph Waldo Emerson

5. Ask students to sign up to bring food, drink, and cups (plastic champagne glasses and sparkling cider are a fun touch) for a party that celebrates one another. This event can be quite meaningful on the last day of school.

Reflection

What acts of kindness have I done lately?

LESSON 3
When Do You Get Your License?

Adolescence

How can I honor the stage of adolescence?

Throughout history Americans in their teens have often played highly responsible roles in their society. They have helped their families survive . . . Young people became teenagers because we had nothing better for them to do. High schools became custodial institutions for the young. We stopped expecting young people to be productive members of the society and began to think of them as gullible consumers . . . What we learn from looking at the past is that there are many different ways in which Americans have been young. Young people and adults need to keep reinventing adolescence so that it serves us all.

—Thomas Hine

Some students sat in my classroom, delighted that they had my undivided attention while they related wild tales of local teenage licentiousness. "You wouldn't want any drug dogs to come to this school's parking lot," they avowed. "Those dogs wouldn't know which way to turn." After assuring me of the overwhelming prevalence of drugs on campus, they turned to stories of weekend revelry. "You would be surprised at the ones who are getting high and having sex," they said. "It's not just the ones you'd think; it's the straight-A students, too." Since they were speaking to me in confidence about their after-hours behavior, I treated the conversation as an opportunity to encourage some reflection, though in my mind I thought about referring this information to administration while keeping the informants anonymous. "Don't you think it's sad that people have to entertain themselves this way?" I asked. One of the students shrugged. "There's nothing to do in this town," he said. "What else are people going to do?"

CULTURAL PHILOSOPHIES

Few teens seem to go untouched by the call of the wild. Many adolescents are depressed, confused, and angry, responding to an overstimulating mass culture offering mostly material or sensuous rituals. Yet our students need to feel as if they are entering young adulthood with honor, pride, and meaning. Many spiritual traditions recognize the sacred nature of the life cycle with several rites of passage, marking the transitions of birth, childhood, coming of age, marriage, aging, and death. The Navajo celebrate a girl's puberty in what is called *kinaalda,* a ceremony full of dancing and music. One component of this ceremony involves eating a large cornmeal cake, while offering small pieces of it to the four cardinal directions and Mother Earth. In some Native American traditions, young men pursue vision quests. In traditional Balinese culture, the tooth-filing ceremony abrades away the animal nature in the youth on the brink of adulthood. The Jewish tradition celebrates the Bar Mitzvah (for young men) and the Bat Mitzvah (for young women), which honor the sacredness of the youth entering adulthood with the support of elders who provide guidance. Though these ceremonies are often public functions, they also recognize the individual's connection with spirit at a certain stage of life. Teaching one another about such rituals can be an uplifting reminder of the meaning already in one's life and an inspiration to create rituals that are not already there.

LESSON IDEAS

1. Use the following questions to spark journal entries and dialogue:

    -   What rituals does your family observe?
    -   What personal rituals do you practice as an individual at significant moments in your life?
    -   What morning or evening, weekday or weekend rituals mark particular moments in your routine, new events in your life, or changes in your attitude?
    -   What is the purpose of rituals? What do they celebrate? What do they teach?

2. Ask for volunteers to share their cultural rites of passage with the class or to invite in family members as guest speakers.

3. Ask students what aspect of their lives needs a ritual to commemorate or appreciate it. Have students break into pairs or work individually to design a ceremony and a ritual object that celebrate an aspect of themselves or their activities. Students can first write out their rituals for your review and then discuss different ways to manufacture the ritual object. I encouraged students to include positive attributes in the ceremony, such as respect for people, places, ideas, or nature. Any method or medium is acceptable for the ritual objects. The individual rituals can be shared or described to the class.

> This activity can precede or follow a more in-depth study of rituals from another culture. When reading *Things Fall Apart* by Chinua Achebe (1959), my students and I re-enacted the scene where the *egwugwu* (elders and spirits of the clan) settle a dispute. We compared the American rituals of robes, gavel, and oath-taking in our court proceedings to the ceremonial masks, staff, and salutes of the Ibo people of Nigeria. Trying to understand the purpose of other cultures' rituals while critically examining our own both lessened the foreign nature of others' practices and highlighted the importance of ritual in everyday life.

> *Adolescence is an age of spiritual hunger and a quest for meaning, as well as a time of tremendous physical and emotional changes. In the Jungian view we are reborn whenever there is the death of an old attitude and the birth of a new consciousness. The spiritual crisis of the adolescent is programmed by biological necessity: death of the dependent child attitudes, rebirth as a psychological adult.*
>
> —Annette Hollander

Reflection

What ritual do I recall that honored my adolescence?

LESSON 4

Respect Others

Respect ∼〰〰〰

How can I expand my students' understanding of respect within a community?

People are people through other people.

—Xhosa saying

The school year began as it always did, with a new crop of students searching for their identities in this community and in some cases testing the classroom boundaries. Before the week was out, one student overstepped what seems to teachers to be an obvious taboo: injuring another student. Snap! went a rubber band, directly into the eye of another student. Ironically, this incident occurred while I was away at human rights education training. When I heard from the substitute what had occurred, I knew what I had to do. I had to speak to the students about compassion and justice while the school year was fresh, and I needed to use language that would be meaningful to them: the importance of their rights and their classmates' rights. The social contract had to be created together, as philosopher John Locke once proposed. He believed that humans in a state of nature will tend to act

129

selfishly and in their own interests, moving quickly toward a state of war with one another. Yet humans will relinquish certain personal freedoms in order to gain security and protection of those rights they deem most essential.

CULTURAL PHILOSOPHIES

All of us exist in relationship with something or someone, and world faiths' greatest teachings ask that our daily interactions with others demonstrate kindness and fairness. A cornerstone in most spiritual traditions is the notion that we are all one and deserve equal reverence. The Jains of India practice *ahisma,* or nonviolence, believing that all things animate and inanimate—stones, rivers, trees, winds, insects, animals, and humans—are considered alive and therefore are to be treated with great respect. Philosopher and ecologist Thomas Berry notes in *Spiritual Literacy,* by Frederic and Mary Ann Brussat (1996), how crucial is the need for us to be reverential: "Every being has its own interior, itself, its mystery, its numinous aspect. To deprive any being of this sacred quality is to disrupt the larger order of the universe. Reverence will be total or it will not be at all" (123). Today with increased awareness of how our smallest actions have ripple effects the world over, people can more easily discuss our global society and human rights violations, speaking to the oneness of human needs and cares that stretch across racial, ethnic, and national lines. In 1948, the United Nations signed the *Universal Declaration of Human Rights,* a document of 30 articles that outlines the fundamental rights to which each person the world over is entitled. Article One makes a powerful beginning: "All human beings are born free and equal in dignity and rights. They are endowed with reason and conscience and should act toward one another in a spirit of brotherhood." More than 150 countries have signed this document, and each nation is continually challenged to live out its principles.

LESSON IDEAS

1. Consider taking time as your class begins a new year or term to ask your students, "How can we create a just, safe, and enjoyable environment for all?" Tell students that one way to approach this

goal is to acknowledge that every person possesses rights under the *Universal Declaration of Human Rights*. Explain the document's history, and have students examine it in detail.

> The *Universal Declaration of Human Rights* is available online in a variety of languages; a short animated film entitled *The Universal Declaration of Human Rights* (Johnson 1988), produced by Amnesty International USA, is another excellent resource.

2. Tell students that the class will be drafting a list of reasonable and necessary rights that all should have in the classroom and that these rights will be posted for all to see. Depending on the group, you can ask students to brainstorm individually or in pairs first. Then lead a whole-class dialogue that allows all ideas to be heard and asks students to elaborate on rights that sound unclear or general.

3. Ask students to find the common themes among their suggestions and create a list of ten or fewer rights. My students have suggested such rights as "I have the right to be heard." "I have the right to be free from harm." "I have the right to learn." "I have the right to be a unique individual." Other ones that are good to include and lead students to are the right to be physically and emotionally safe, the right to speak or work without interruption, and the right to be treated seriously.

4. After the students write the list, have them create a poster displaying the list and have everyone sign the document. Post it in a highly visible place. Use it as a reference point for grounding students when they forget their commitment to this contract.

5. To further explore human rights issues, gather students around a map of the world. Examine it to identify areas where students believe that human rights violations or advances in human rights are occurring. Depending on your subject, assign a project that challenges your students to explore the principles of the declaration in depth. See the project ideas below.

   Art: Students can make a tribute to the declaration in the tradition of Tibetan Buddhist prayer flags. These flags hang in the mountain passes, carrying blessings and supplications in the wind. Printed on each flag are prayers for long life, prosperity,

> For further ideas of how to create a social contract with your class, consult Judy Anderson's book, *Social Contract—What We Believe* (1996).

and good luck as well as a windhorse, or *lung-ta*, to carry the message to the deities. Have each student draw an illustration depicting the text of one of the articles, using markers or block print stamps on 12-inch squares of cotton fabric. Use the colors of white, green, yellow, red, and blue, each representing the five elements of ether, water, earth, fire, and air, respectively. If fabric is not available, construction paper with collages or decorative writing will also work. Attach these flags in a chain so they can flutter in the wind outside your school or hang across a hallway or on walls.

English, history, or foreign language: As you study a particular novel, country, or period of history, ask your students to research incidents or scour the texts you study for incidents that specifically violate one or more articles of the declaration. Search also for human rights advances. Each student can present her findings to the class. During the unit, students can draw inspiration from watching the PBS special, *A Force More Powerful*, which chronicles Gandhi's and American civil rights leaders' use of nonviolent passive resistance in fighting injustice.

Where, after all, do universal rights begin? In small places, close to home—so close and so small that they cannot be seen on any maps of the world . . . Such are the places where every man, woman and child seeks equal justice, equal opportunity, equal dignity without discrimination. Unless these rights have meaning there, they have little meaning anywhere.

—Eleanor Roosevelt

Reflection

How do I demonstrate respect for others within my community?

LESSON 5

You Are Behaving Like Animals!

Reverence

How can I teach reverence for all creatures?

"It seems fairly obvious to some of us that a lot of scholars need to go outside and sniff around—walk through the grass, talk to the animals. That sort of thing . . .

"Lots of people talk to animals," said Pooh.

"Maybe, but . . ."

"Not very many listen, though," he said.

"That's the problem," he added.

—Benjamin Hoff, *The Tao of Pooh*

One day in the middle of class I saw a spider walking across the floor. I paused and carefully picked it up with a piece of paper. I opened the door leading outside and released it safely into a more suitable environment. A student looked at me and said,

"Hey, why are you doing that? I usually step on them."

"Why?" I asked.

"Well, it's just a bug, and it's small—what does it matter?" he said.

"Does a creature's size matter in the natural world?" I asked. "Does this small spider have any less right to live than a lion?"

"Well, no, if you put it like that," the student responded sheepishly. Ironically, this student probably returned home to his dog that same day and lavished it with affection.

Many of us could describe the joys and antics of our pets. We are constantly entertained and mystified by the animals in our lives. My cat Abby has taught me a lesson or two that I should heed. If you want something, be persistent. Stretch frequently. Gaze intently. Be independent and rest as needed. One teacher I know helps her homeroom bond on the first day of classes by discussing pets, and her great enthusiasm for her own menagerie brings delight to everyone else. I engage regularly in animal adoration until I encounter pets that are unfamiliar or aren't, as the environmental movement has joked, "charismatic megafauna." The practices of modern industrialization tend to keep the animal kingdom at bay behind zoo walls, in parks, in preserved collections, or as objects for scientific study and testing. Many creatures are feared and misunderstood, rather than sought out as sources of great learning and sacred life.

CULTURAL PHILOSOPHIES

The word "animal" comes from the Latin word *animalis,* which means animate, deriving from the Latin *anima,* meaning breath or soul. Although some people dispute that animals have souls, some who work closely with animals believe otherwise, such as those who have witnessed dolphins working patiently with disabled children, swimming alongside them in controlled environments. Numerous stories abound about pets miraculously saving their owners' lives or providing healing through their mere presence. Contact with these animals in "pet therapy," even for short periods of time, is said to alleviate depression and bring enjoyment to patients.

Certain Native American cultures believe in the interconnectedness of all beings, and that all creatures and things, animate or inanimate, coexist with energy or spirit. Certain prayers address the animals, from the four-leggeds to the two-leggeds. The white buffalo is considered sacred by some Native American nations and represents a sign that prayers are being heard. Many Pacific Northwest tribes make bowls carved with forms of totem animals, such as bear, raven, and killer whale, and the Zuni of the Southwest carve animal fetishes, running a heart line from the mouth through the heart, representing how what we take into our hearts we give back to the world. The majority of indigenous cultures have trusted that animals can be our educators, believing that characteristics of certain animals illustrate traits in us that need to be developed. These guardian spirits—also called power animals, totem animals, or animal helpers—are seen as strong spirits, sometimes even as part of the tribe. Throughout a lifetime, a person should honor his animal helper for the gifts and guidance it provides. Usually an animal will choose a person, and though this totem animal may initially be frightening, these fears can also be teachers. Some cultures believe that if an animal has ever bitten you, your totem is testing your abilities to handle the special qualities it presents.

Many cultures value animals spiritually: St. Francis of Assisi, a Catholic monk who lived during the 13th century, called animals "brother" and "sister." In Hindu tradition, two extremely popular gods are the elephant-headed Ganesha and the monkey Hanuman. Hanuman, a divine monkey devotee of Rama, is an incarnation of Vishnu, one of the deities of the Hindu trinity of Brahma, Shiva, and Vishnu.

LESSON IDEAS

1. To encourage students to develop awareness and understanding of the animal kingdom, have them research and create an art project that embraces a deep understanding of our natural world. Ask each student to pick a nondomesticated animal that she has an affinity for and to learn all that she can about that animal. Students can study different animals through traditional research, zoo visits, or interviews, depending on your community resources. Encourage students to think beyond familiar animals, seeking out those found on other continents or in other geographical locations.

Valuable resources to consult are *Through Other Eyes: Animal Stories by Women* (Zahava 1988), *When Elephants Weep* (McCarthy and Masson 1996), or *Animal Speak* (Andrews 1994).

2. Ask students to consider why the animals they chose speak to them. They might use the following questions as a starting point:

   - What adjectives come to mind when I look at this animal and read about its characteristics?
   - What are some strengths and weaknesses of this animal?
   - What type of environment does this animal live in?
   - What does this animal symbolize in our culture? In other cultures?
   - How can this animal teach me about my own strengths and weaknesses?
   - Does any aspect of this animal frighten me? What can that fear teach me?

3. Have students create a collage or a sculpture of their chosen animal. When they are finished, ask for volunteers to present their works of art and answers to the questions above.

4. Students may also wish to share tales of the amazing connections they feel with animals and animal feats they have witnessed. Many will share fond anecdotes of the healing that animals have provided in their lives.

> *If you talk to the animals, they will talk with you, and you will know each other. If you do not talk to them, you will not know them, and what you do not know you will fear. What one fears one destroys.*
>
> —Chief Dan George

Reflection

What animal has something to teach me about reverence?

These Are a Few of My Favorite Things

Love

How can I encourage students to explore the many expressions and essence of love?

We are shaped and fashioned by what we love.
—Johann Wolfgang Von Goethe

People tend to stop for a moment when they learn what my profession is and say, "Oh, you're a teacher? Wow. I could never do that." Most assuredly, there are days when I wonder whether I can. Some nights I come home so exhausted I'm shaking. My head is throbbing. My movements are fumbling at best. I ask myself, "Why on earth did I choose this job?" Sometimes I'm not even sure what it is that happened that day that was so tiring; I am simply spent. Once when I lamented how I had little time and energy to do volunteer work beyond school, a colleague commented, "You know, teaching is our charity work." She was right. So much of a teacher's life is spent healing and helping myriad children. We feed them when they are

hungry; we give them a pencil and paper when they have none. Outside the classroom, we are on the fields and courts watching students' victories; we are in the hallways listening to their stories; and we are in the community, hugging them after several months and years, joyful at the sight of a former student who shares incredible memories with us. We give the kind of love and encouragement that parents and friends can't always give. Sometimes, others will remind us of our gifts, like the parent who called me for an appointment and instead of bringing a concern, brought me a bouquet of flowers and a warm thank you. I was deeply moved by her gesture, and I told myself, *Remember this moment.* This is a symbol of the love we give coming back to us. And we are better people for having loved the youths who keep us honest and awake and learning.

CULTURAL PHILOSOPHIES

A celebration of love is usually relegated to one day of the year, with a focus on the romantic aspects of love, but educators have the ability and opportunity to celebrate love every day. Krishnamurti, a spiritual teacher of the Hindu tradition, explains how teachers can express a simple and tender love that encourages a person to be gentle to all things. The educator imparts not only information about such subjects as mathematics and geography but also communicates this love when she works, plays, or eats with a student. He writes, "It is very important to talk about love, to feel it, to nourish it, to treasure it, otherwise it is soon dissipated, for the world is very brutal" (Krishnamurti 1953, 192). Spiritual traditions speak of a transcendent love—the love of God, love for all people, love for every creature on this earth. Mother Teresa was a living example of such love in action. Her compassion touched all corners of the world, teaching others the beauty and simplicity of unconditional sacrifice for others. In his book *The Way of Love,* Jesuit priest Anthony De Mello (1991) speaks to this kind of love that accepts everyone no matter what their imperfections. He asks, "What is love? Take a look at a rose. Is it possible for the rose to say, 'I shall offer my fragrance to good people and withhold from bad people?'. . . And observe how helplessly and indiscriminately a tree gives its shade to everyone, good and bad, young and old, high and low, animals and humans and every living creature even to the one who seeks to cut it down" (107). And like the tree and the rose there exists a second quality of love—gratuitousness—to give and ask for nothing in return. This kind of "gift love" and "appreciative love," which writer C. S. Lewis (1960) notes in his explorations of the four loves—affection, friendship, eros, and charity—is the divine being's love for its creation. Many faiths instruct humans to seek the divine with such a love. In Sufism, or *tasawwuf,* the mystical branch of Islam, one seeks union with the beloved, which is Allah. Sufism recognizes only one God, who is the God of all people and all true religions and draws upon the wisdom of the great prophets, which include Jesus, Moses, David, Solomon, Abraham, and Mohammed. At the essence of Sufism is the realization of the current of love that unifies all life as one people, one ecology, one universe, and one being. Viewing love as the highest intelligence, Sufis seek a path of sharing selfless love with the world. In the past 14 centuries of Sufi writing, the love described is not the feel-good, temporary experience but a deep union of hearts that goes beyond any romantic concept. Such was the love that moved the spirit of the well-known 13th-century Sufi poet Jelaluddin Rumi, who, in a state of grief at the loss of his teacher Shams, began turning around a pole. He held on with one uplifted arm and the other extended outward in an expression of love, pouring forth his poetry in a passionate expression of breath and movement. Today, the whirling dervishes still turn in Rumi's honor, as an act of bringing body and soul into unity with the universe. Today, the Dances of Universal Peace, founded in Sufism, integrate movement and breath to awaken the message of love.

LESSON IDEAS

1. In class, initiate a discussion to clarify the differences in meaning among words such as "love," "like," "dislike," and "hate." Put a controversial statement on the board: "The word 'love' is used too casually nowadays." Ask students about their observations and opinions regarding this subject, and a lively conversation will probably ensue.

2. Ask students to explore the depth of the word "love" by creating a private list of 40 people, experiences, or things that they love. Encourage students to remember all the joys their senses bring them in the smallest moments of the day.

At first students may struggle with finding things to list. When I tried this activity, I noticed that students started to catalogue each family member, including aunts, uncles, cousins, second cousins, and so on in a grocery-list fashion. With some further discussion, students realized that there are many sensory, emotional, intellectual, and spiritual experiences to celebrate, such as seeing the color of the sky at sunset, or touching a baby's skin, or seeing pride or joy in someone's eyes. These moments might best be described with the word "love."

3. Then ask them to select some favorites and answer this question: How do the things you love express who you are?

4. While they write, play Chopin, Mozart, or any particular composer or musical form that you love. Encourage students to look deeper into their experience and recount soulful moments that were joyful and filled with deep feeling, whether fleeting or long term. Consider also listening to recorded poetry that expresses so eloquently the loves of the ages, and encourage the students to discuss the different types of passion expressed in each.

Nurturing the soul requires an openness to love's many forms.
—Thomas Moore

Reflection

How do I experience and express love's essence in my life?

Have You Hugged a Tree Lately?

Compassion ~~~~

How can I encourage my students to develop compassion for nature?

Walk through an old oak grove, piney woods, apple orchard, or ancient redwood forest and you discover how easy it is to be overcome by the quiet majesty of trees. They supply shelter and nourishment to many of earth's creatures. They purify our air and give us shade.

—Maggy Howe

One year I was shocked by an incident of vandalism at our school. Someone girdled the young oak tree given to our school as a gift, scraping away enough bark in hopes of ensuring a certain death. Few students reacted to the event with concern or outrage; one even wondered what the big deal was, since in his eyes a tree wasn't "a living thing." I was deeply disturbed. The act took on symbolic significance for me, as a sign of "kids today." As a teacher I knew that my response to our tree dying had to be outspoken and symbolic in itself: If I did

not express my concern, then I was accepting the desecration of the tree. I felt our school needed a healing ceremony. I approached one of my classes that I thought might be open to such a suggestion.

I first encouraged students to explore writings about nature. Then they copied lines of poetry and personal reflections on nature onto multicolored strips of fabric. We went outside, gathered around the tree, and wrapped it with the strips of cloth. Soon the trunk was bound with a woven scarf of pink and blue and green and yellow, and we could no longer see the marks of the girdling. Then we read aloud from a book of poetry about nature. Students enjoyed this process as well as being part of a healing ceremony that was visible for all to see. Worn by weather, the strips remained for many months.

CULTURAL PHILOSOPHIES

Modern Western society has steadily denied its natural impulses and connections with nature for several hundred years. Some people have comfortably adopted the philosophy that nature is our property to use however we like. Many cultures around the world, however, have valued nature—trees in particular—from the earliest times to present day. In Native American and Celtic traditions, the tree represents the unification of earth and heaven as it grows upwards. Trees are thought to communicate with the wind, stars, and moon. Any warnings or heavenly messages are sent by the wind and travel down the trunk to the roots. To receive guidance, a person need only sit at the trunk of the tree and ask the tree spirit for help. The Celtic tradition honored nine types of trees as sacred for their properties and medicinal purposes: willow, rowan, pine, elm, birch, hazel, yew, holly, and oak. Festivals were celebrated with fires using each of these types of wood. Today, sacred woods and groves can still be found in India, Bali, Africa, and Japan, similar to those that existed in pre-Christian Europe. In Greek mythology, the oak tree was sacred to Zeus, and in Ancient Egypt the sycamore carried special mythical importance. Buddha meditated under the pipal tree until he attained enlightenment. In Genesis, the tree of life and the tree of knowledge of good and evil grow in the center of the Garden of Eden. The acacia tree, native of Africa, was used to build the Ark of the Covenant and is mentioned by the prophet Isaiah as a sign of Messianic restoration in Israel. The acacia's deep roots and survival of drought and famine make it not only a biblical symbol but also a symbol of the land of Africa. The lote tree symbolizes for Muslims the boundary between the human and the divine. Today in South India, there is a pilgrimage to the forest, which is a place called Sabarimala. Hundreds of thousands of people make the pilgrimage yearly, seeing the journey as a return to a time before they were settled in homes and cities, a time to reconnect to the forest, to the wild, and to the past. Some indigenous peoples, such as certain Native American shamans, have viewed trees and plants as sources of life that need to be respected. When shamans seek a medicinal cure, they first ask the plant for its gift of curative powers. The knowledge that people across the world have rich cultural traditions of valuing nature can make us pause and wonder why we have lost such appreciation. Our students aren't so far from frolicking in mud puddles and rolling in the grass. They can easily be reminded that the chasm drawn between humanity and the rest of the natural world is false. They can open their hearts to restoring an appreciation of nature.

LESSON IDEAS

1. Discuss with your students the ways your school community treats and relates to the natural areas on campus. Are there trees, and if so, how are they treated? Are there places that could benefit from more natural beauty? If so, what could your class do to beautify them and "bring nature back"?

2. Respond to any mistreatment of nature with a class project. Ask the students to think of ways to heal in response to vandalism or cruelty.

3. Even if nature hasn't been damaged, you can still encourage respect by taking students right to the source—a forest—to see, hear, feel, taste, and smell their interconnectedness with other living things. Prepare students by showing them one of artist Andy Goldsworthy's several books with photographs of the art he creates using only nature.

4. Ask students to find poems and writings that reflect the human connection to the earth or write their own. They can transfer their poems to fabric by writing with permanent marker on multicolored fabric in at least one-yard lengths. Have students read aloud their writing and other chosen poetry as the spirit moves them while

enjoying the shade and presence of the tree. Students might also be inspired to create a natural sculpture, in the style of Andy Goldsworthy, or wrap a tree without making a significant impact on the environment. Encourage your students to make their artwork blend with and complement the natural scenery. Once they have finished their creations, ask students to share their feelings with the group.

- How did you feel during this process?
- How would you describe your relationship with nature during this process?
- How do these rituals benefit you and the group as a whole?
- How does this experience compare with your previous experiences being outdoors?
- What do you notice most when you are outdoors?
- How does spending time outdoors affect you? Does it inspire you? In what way?
- How do you see yourself when you are outdoors?
- What is your role in the natural environment?
- Would you like to spend more time in nature? Why or why not?
- What other artists or writers have used nature as a source of inspiration?

> *And this, our life, exempt from public haunt, finds tongues in trees, books in the running brooks, sermons in stones, and good in everything.*
>
> —William Shakespeare, *As You Like It* (II, i)

Reflection

How can I deepen my compassion for nature?

LESSON 8

Just Be Yourself

Self-Awareness ~~~~

How can I encourage my students to find their strengths within their weaknesses?

The world is round and the place which may seem like the end may also be only the beginning.

—Ivy Baker Priest

One of my former students recounts to me how desperate and tortured she was in the first year of middle school. Mocked and bullied from all sides, she wondered if it would simply be better if her life ended. I look at her now, blossomed into a luminescent, accomplished young woman who believes in herself wholeheartedly and makes new friends easily. She is such a radiant, soulful person that it is hard to imagine her feeling so depressed or that anyone ever strove to make her life miserable. But when I hear her story, I understand that part of her luminescence has a foundation in her trials. The fires of her life refined her into a brighter shade of gold.

CULTURAL PHILOSOPHIES

We all know the story of the ugly duckling. How easily and often adolescents can parrot what others have said about them: I'm stupid; I'm a dreamer; I'm not good enough. What a crime! As the philosopher Michel de Montaigne once wrote: "Of all the infirmities we have, the most savage is to despise our being." At the core of every person is the need to recognize strengths and to put to rest harmful messages that attack self-esteem. If we can find the strength in our weakness, we can define ourselves in our own way with greater awareness and joy. The yin-yang symbol of the Daoist philosophy represents the frequent paradox of our lives: two opposite states of being that are ubiquitous and complementary. Contained in the Dao, or Great Ultimate, are yin and yang. Yin designates all things dark, cold, earthly, feminine, passive, retiring, and receptive; yang symbolizes what is bright, hot, heavenly, masculine, active, and expansive. In the white segment of the circular symbol a spot of black appears, and in the black segment, a spot of white, signifying that everything is composed of both yin and yang. Nature perfectly illustrates the transformation of phenomena at their greatest intensity into their antithesis. Cold follows hot in the seasonal cycle, while a storm's prelude and finale is a great calm. Historians and educators alike joke about the pendulum swing of human decisions in both politics and education reform. But a Daoist can find peace among such vacillations, knowing that the more things change, the more they stay the same; bad times give way to good. In this cyclical balancing act, neither yin nor yang dominates. Power and submission, wealth and poverty, and wellness and sickness are constantly exchanging places in the universal dance of life. Thus a person practicing T'ai Chi movements seeks balance, not extreme positioning. Daoists seek to live harmoniously with the circumstances of everyday life, finding serenity and sweetness in what others might perceive as chaotic or sour.

LESSON IDEAS

1. Explore the meaning of the yin-yang symbol with your students. Ask them to look at the symbol and tell you not what they might know or assume about the symbol's meaning but simply what they see: colors, lines, shapes, and so forth. The principle of balance

will soon emerge. List some of the words associated with yin and yang. Some students may express concern that "feminine" is associated with "passive," "cold" and "retiring," assuming that these are negative qualities. Challenge those assumptions; ask students what are the positive aspects of these qualities. Though the Dao may group these qualities together, the overall point of the symbol is balance, where a greater whole is achieved in having encompassed all. Then ask students to volunteer examples of how they see these principles play out in daily life.

2. Tell students they will now look at the yin, the yang, and the Dao within themselves in order to find the strength in their weakness. First they can practice by looking at some characters, objects, or concepts they have recently been studying to see how these possess double-sided qualities. For example, a character's outspokenness may be her blessing in one situation and her curse in another; a certain element or plant might have a certain property or characteristic that both strengthens and weakens it. Many of history's most impractical dreamers were also our most visionary thinkers. What are the yin, yang, and Dao of an atom? Ask students to list their opposite qualities that coexist as well as negative qualities that can be seen in a positive light.

3. Ask the class to brainstorm a list of negative words used to describe people every day: irresponsible, lazy, weird, selfish, and so forth. Then challenge students in groups of two or three to convert these words into new ones that emphasize the positive. Ask students to provide examples of how this new word applies. For example, a selfish person might actually be self-directed, or a person with boundaries who knows when to say no. A reckless person might be courageous; a loner, independent; a weird person, original.

4. Have each student make a personal list of negatives attributed to him as labels and turn them into positives. Students can reflect on these qualities in a journal entry:

   - What negative words have been used to describe me?
   - What positive words can replace these, showing another way of looking at what might be considered negative?
   - Which of these qualities is predominant in my character?

Some of my students wrote the following about themselves: stuck-up became confident; pessimistic became grounded; and goofy became uplifting. My two favorites, perhaps because I knew the lovable and sassy characters who wrote them, were "short = I am good at squeezing through tight places" and "annoying = Hey, I'm persistent!"

- In what situations does this quality become a benefit and when does it become a liability?
- How can I balance the strength and the weakness of this quality?

5. Ask if there are volunteers who would not mind standing up and sharing their new look at a "flaw." For further exploration of Daoism, consider having your students read excerpts from *The Tao of Pooh* (1982), by Benjamin Hoff.

As human beings, our greatness lies not so much in being able to remake the world . . . as in being able to remake ourselves.

—Mahatma Gandhi

Reflection

How can I be gentler with my weaknesses?

Tell Me about Yourself

Individuality

How can I encourage students to explore and celebrate their unique qualities?

> *To have one's individuality completely ignored is like being pushed quite out of life. Like being blown out as one blows out a light.*
>
> —Evelyn Scott

The summer before my freshman year in college, I was recuperating from a stressful senior year in high school. Physically and mentally depleted, I stayed close to home and mulled over the impending college experience. I was scared. I had no idea who my new friends would be, what my classes would demand, what my daily routine would look like. As I languished in my room, listening to music, an art project materialized. I took a clear plastic clipboard and began to cover it with images of myself: popular sayings that spoke to me, celebrities I idolized, photos of best friends, and lines from favorite movies and

authors. I spent hours and hours creating it. Now, looking back, I see how I was searching for certainty about who I was on the brink of a life-altering experience; I needed confirmation of my individuality, psyche, and spirit at this stage of life. I would carry this clipboard with me to college almost as a proud and defiant shield, as if to say, "Hey, this is me, and don't you forget it!"

CULTURAL PHILOSOPHIES

Student chatter may seem superficial, limited to entertainment and clothing and gossip, but if we give students a chance to tell us more about themselves, they will show their depth, from dreams to fears. This search for wholeness, for connection, for knowing oneself drives every human soul. The primary question along a spiritual path is "Who am I?" Hinduism speaks of the Atman, or eternal self, that is one with Brahman. Christianity states "the kingdom of God is within you," while Buddhists may say, "You are the Buddha." If we view education as a spiritual journey, the primary goal should be to discover the self in all its manifestations: emotional, physical, mental, and spiritual.

LESSON IDEAS

1. Ask students to create symbolic collages in honor of self. These are representative portraits of the self-defining activities, people, objects, and experiences in students' lives. Explain to them that they will be creating a collage of all that holds special meaning to them.

2. Ask students to write privately in answer to this question: Who or what makes me what I am? Encourage them to think beyond the initial responses of material possessions to the more deeply felt qualities of heritage, culture, belief, personal aspirations, and passions. After they have thought privately about words, ask them to begin thinking about visual images that reflect these qualities.

3. Have students start with a sheet of 18" x 24" drawing paper. In the center of the collage, they should put a photograph of themselves. School photos often work well. Surrounding the photo, they can place images representing important events and experiences. Challenge them to use a variety of media, found objects (including three-dimensional objects), mementos, photos, clippings, and paint.

4. Invite students to share their work with the class and tell the story behind a picture:

    - This experience/event/item is special to me because . . .
    - I believe deeply in . . .
    - My passion is . . .
    - An important moment in my life was . . .

> *Become aware of what is in you. Announce it, pronounce it, produce it and give birth to it.*
> —Meister Eckhart, German mystic

Reflection

How can I celebrate my unique qualities?

LESSON 10
Did You Say You're Sorry?

Forgiveness

How can I help my students understand the power of compassion and forgiveness?

Life appears to me too short to be spent in nursing animosity or registering wrong.

—Charlotte Brontë

As a student teacher I taught in a challenging third-grade classroom. These kids were toughened by life, and fights started frequently throughout the school, including in my classroom. In this class were three boys who, despite being seated at opposite ends of the room, would continually break into screaming matches. Finally I'd had it. The school counselor was overwhelmed, and I knew that if these boys ended up in his office, they would simply be assigned detention. So I quickly gathered the three of them. "Grab a chair," I said, "and listen to what I have to say." I hustled them and the chairs into the hallway. First I tried to give them some insight into their behavior, sage advice that seemed to bounce right off them. Then, in a moment of inspiration, I said, "It's time for some art." I asked each boy to make a very special card that he would give his best friend. I asked them to think about what they would say, and how much a good friendship meant to them, and how all friends appreciate receiving a card. I saw relief in their eyes, and I knew they were thinking, "Hey, this isn't so bad." The real test came when I returned and asked them to exchange their cards in the hallway. They were stunned. But after a short discussion of the value of friendship and forgiveness, they agreed, and somewhat reluctantly, each handed the boy next to him a handmade card.

CULTURAL PHILOSOPHIES

Throughout the day, students absorb much negativity: teasing from others, disappointments in love or friendship, and defeats in a classroom or on an athletic field. Poisoned by anger and humiliation, a student can wallow in pain that seeks an outlet. We can help students move beyond past events by helping them to erase the board to make room for positive thoughts and gratitude. Such is the basis of a successful practice in schools known as *restitution*. The major focus of restitution is helping the offender align her actions with her vision of herself as a caring, responsible individual. This ongoing process of making amends to the victim as well as healing oneself is truly an act of creativity. Based on several experts' studies, the theory of restitution rests on five principles, which can be found in detail in *Restitution: Restructuring School Discipline* (1996), *Restitution Triangle* (1996), and *Resolving Conflict Using Restitution* (1999), all by Diane Gossen. Restitution helps a student ask what kind of a person he wishes to be. To rebuild his self-image, he must take action to restore the self. Forgiving allows one to focus energy on redemption while surrendering the ego judgment of self and others.

LESSON IDEAS

1. When a student does wrong, reflect on what opportunities you can create for the student to reflect on and redeem the situation. Author Perry Good's *In Pursuit of Happiness* (1996) and Diane Gossen's publications offer many helpful questions to help a student

evaluate her goals and actions in terms of consequences for self and community. A student can also reflect on how her actions create a change in the classroom and school community.

2. If the community is affected by an act that requires forgiveness, consider asking students to complete journal entries exploring this event and the ideas of mercy and exoneration. Forgiveness is taught in many spiritual traditions, just as the Golden Rule is, and you can use the quotations at the bottom of the page to focus a dialogue.

3. Consider a journal prompt that allows students to explore a personal case in which forgiveness is needed. They can write "the letter they'll never send," a letter to someone in their lives (parent, relative, teacher, coach, sibling, friend) who needs to hear something from them. In the past, my students have begun their

Hindu: *If you want to see the brave, look at those who can forgive. If you want to see the heroic, look at those who can love in return for hatred.*

—Bhagavad-Gita 14:23

Buddhist: *For never does hatred cease by hatred here below; hatred ceases by love; this is an eternal law.*

—Dhammapada 5

Christian: *And forgive us our debts, as we also have forgiven our debtors. . . . For if you forgive men their trespasses, your heavenly Father also will forgive you.*

—Matthew 6:12, 14 (Holy Bible, New International version)

Muslim: *Saying a word that is kind and forgiving is better than charity that hurts.*

—Al-Qur'an 2:263

Jewish: *If your enemy is hungry, give him bread to eat. If he is thirsty, give him water to drink. You will be heaping live coals on his head, and the Lord will reward you.*

—The Holy Scriptures, Proverbs 25:21–22

letters with such powerful lines as, "Dear Coach, would you please give us a break? I think you hate us," and "Dear Friend, I can't forgive you for lying to me all the time." I always allow students the option of privacy by permitting them to fold over a page they prefer I not view. For those who openly share pain that shows they are endangered, I explain to them my legal and moral duty to refer them to a counselor. Teachers must always be prepared when initiating such a journal prompt that certain students will cry out for help, whether they will consciously admit it as such. Whether students appreciate the intervention or not, I make sure that they know how important their safety and healing is to me.

4. Often historical, literary, or current events that students encounter expose violent ways of resolving painful feelings. These incidents and the characters involved offer opportunities for students to dialogue about other approaches to healing dissension and its wounds. Students may wish to write a letter that a character might have written to understand her own feelings before taking a certain action or they may want to write a new ending to the tale.

5. Explore historical examples of forgiveness that attempt to provide healing within a culture. Powerful paradigm shifts such as South Africa's Truth and Reconciliation Act testify to humanity's creative power to make strides toward, forgiveness, restitution, and healing after years of injustice and inhumanity.

> *there is no answer*
> *but loving one another,*
> *even our enemies, and this is hard.*
> —Wendell Berry

Reflection

How can I practice forgiveness and compassion?

Appendix

Meditations, Prompts, and Student Examples

What's for Lunch? Meditations and Prompts

Eating Meditation Script I

Read the following passage from *One Day in the Life of Ivan Denisovich* (Solzhenitsyn 1998), pausing halfway through to ask students to begin eating: "He reached for the hunk of bread, wrapped in a piece of clean cloth, and, holding the cloth at chest level so that not a crumb should fall to the ground, began to nibble and chew at the bread. The bread, which he had carried under two garments, had been warmed by his body. The frost hadn't caught it at all . . . You had to eat with all your mind on the food—like now, nibbling at the bread bit by bit, working the crumbs up into a paste with your tongue and sucking it into your cheeks. And how good it tasted—that soggy black bread! . . . Shukhov ate his bread down to his very fingers, keeping only a little bit of bare crust, the half-moon-shaped top of the loaf—because no spoon is as good for scraping a bowl of cereal clean as a bread crust. He wrapped the crust in his cloth again and slipped it into his inside pocket for dinner." (55–57)

Eating Meditation Script II

Adapt the following meditation to whatever food you will use. This meditation is written for an orange: *Unpeel the rind. Notice the process as it unfolds. What does the orange feel like? What does it smell like? What is required to arrive at the center of the orange? Once you arrive at the core, continue to eat the orange in silence, still paying attention to the taste, smells, textures, as well as the method of eating and chewing. As you chew, imagine all the steps of an orange's growth, from seedling to tree to fruit; imagine all the hands that helped bring this food to life and to you, from the process of planting to that of nourishing, picking, loading, delivering, and selling. Visualize the vitamins and nutritive properties of an orange sustaining your body.*

Journal Prompt

The spiritual philosophy of Zen Buddhism teaches mindfulness in all aspects of one's life. Try eating something simple (such as a piece of bread or fruit) and eating it very slowly, paying close attention to every detail of the experience. Note your sensory responses (sight, smell, taste, touch, hearing) and any other responses (emotional, intellectual, spiritual) that you have to this experience.

Student Responses

Garrett wrote: "As the grain bread enters my mouth it enters as a foreign object. It is a new substance and therefore it must be tested. Its texture is soft and it is easily pressed to the roof of my mouth, my tongue feeling its many holes and pores. Then with a flick of the tongue, the bread is brought back into the main chamber of my mouth. I exhale. The taste begins to fill my mouth. It is wholesome and leaves me wanting more. I begin to pass the bread from one side of my mouth to the other. As the urge to swallow becomes stronger, I fight it; I don't want the experience to end. Quickly the bread is dissolving. What has happened to the original chunk? Soon I am left with nothing but a memory and this piece of paper."

Alex wrote: "The value of food becomes lost in our society where hunger is not a problem . . . The whole experience is not the same for privileged people whose material dreams are of fancy cars and computers and technology . . . As I thought some more as I ate, I thought about the path the apple took on the way from where it was grown to my mouth and all the work it took to get that apple, and it seemed a little more special. I believe that we can only really appreciate food after we are forced to go without it."

Student Responses to Grace Prompts in OK, You Can Have an Extension

Simran: "Grace is absolute forgiveness. In my view, I would add on that grace is a forgiveness in a peaceful way with no hard feelings. I do have a spiritual belief that believes in grace. Sikhism is a monotheistic religion that not many people may know about. Only about 23 million Sikhs live in the world today. People who do bad deeds, if they are Sikhs, are given grace by helping others. If a man kills someone, he can be given grace by helping others throughout his life."

Mike: "Grace is a word for forgiveness or a favor that has religious connotations. I do not have any religious beliefs. My family is the oddest I have ever known religious-wise. My mother and stepfather are Buddhists, I am atheist, my father is Baptist, and my brother is Catholic and studies Catholicism. I have not yet given my brother grace for being born. For a long time I wished he hadn't been and treated him thus, so I guess in fact it's me that needs grace from him."

Bonnye: "It's really hard to have religious tolerance for me. As a child I grew up Southern Baptist . . . and the rules were strict. Pity those who are not of your religion but *never* marry or befriend for they can make you stray. I think that "better than thou" attitude is what sent me to Wicca. No, it's not "witchcraft," it's more than that. Through Wicca I've learned a lot about tolerance and forgiveness. Wicca teaches each person chooses their own path of religion and it is *not* your place to pass judgment. What is right for you is not always right for someone else. But, because of these differences you are to show kindness and understanding towards other religions. Because of my new ideas I've been called a lot of things. I've been told I was Satanist and God was going to throw me down to the fires of hell. Ignorance. It's hard to forgive these hypocrites. Don't their own laws say treat others as you want to be treated? No man is without sin? Basic understanding and curiosity seem muddled under the blanket of Christianity. But, through it all I struggle to show grace and try to understand where the ignorance and misunderstanding comes in, hard as it may be. Every one deserves a second chance."

Jonathan: "I think that grace, through Judaism, can be/is very important to me. The night before Yom Kippur, the most important Jewish holiday, is Kol Nidre. I don't know the exact translation of it, but it represents the Covenant every Jew holds with God. The Kol Nidre service is very somber, and basically what occurs is that God gives you grace. For every promise you made but couldn't keep, for every sin you've committed, you are forgiven. You start the new Jewish year with a clean slate. In my mind, that exactly meshes with the definition of grace— absolute forgiveness and being given a clean slate. I suppose it's more of the Catholic definition, because you ask God for forgiveness. I don't know enough theology to know if you are forgiven if you don't ask for it. So, in my mind, the most important part of the most important holiday really makes grace essential to my beliefs."

Justin: "I believe that grace is the period of time in which people would be forgiven for their wrongdoings and be given another chance. As a Buddhist, I would say that there is grace, but we would have to find a way to repent for our wrongdoing and that our guilty conscience would be harder to get rid of from our mind."

Megan: "Grace, in my religion . . . is better known as atonement. I'm a Mormon. Mormons are Christians, contrary to popular belief, as is evidenced by the principle of atonement. The basic Christian knowledge is that Jesus Christ was God's only begotten, was the perfect man, and died for the sins of mankind. Now, many other Christian denominations believe that all you have to do to access this gift of grace (He died that man may be saved) is confess your sins to a priest or pastor and shout out a few Hail Marys. My spiritual belief is in the process of repentance. Mormon doctrine teaches five steps of repentance in order to obtain grace: feeling true sorrow (i.e., recognizing what you did was wrong and *wanting* to repent), confession (either to the Lord or, in serious cases, to the bishop), restitution (doing the best you can to fix/make it better), and never doing it again. Only when these four steps are honestly and wholeheartedly completed is one fully forgiven and their 'sins, though they be crimson red shall be made the purest white.'"

Cyrus: "Grace: the act of total forgiveness and understanding, a way to wipe the slate clean. My spiritual beliefs at the time do not involve the act of grace, since I don't really have a spiritual belief system. However, forgiveness is one of my morals. One small example of grace I can remember springs from my younger days as a spry young whipper-snapper. One day at my friend's house, we decided that it would be a good idea to shoot his dog. So we did, with water guns, mind you. His mother soon burst onto the scene and stopped us. So we argued with her. Finally she gave us grace and wiped our dirty slate clean. This petty little anecdote is but a metaphor for the grace that sometimes exists in our world. When I was given this grace I felt pretty sorry, but that soon passed. A person in my life that could use some grace right now is my sister. She angers me with her lack of respect for me and her vicious attitude. I find it hard to forgive my sibling from time to time, but I think if I tried I could."

You Are Safe Here Meditation Script

We will begin now by taking slow deep breaths . . . Breathe in and fill your lungs with air and slowly exhale . . . Begin to become aware of your breath . . . Notice the deep inhalation as your lungs fill with air and the soft exhalation as the breath leaves your body . . . [**Allow at least five deep breaths before proceeding.**] *Now imagine a place where you feel safe . . . It can be a place you know or a place you would like to visit . . . It could be a beach . . . a forest or park . . . or a place of safety at home . . . Imagine all the sensations of this place . . . If you are at the beach, notice the warmth of the sun on your face and the sea mist in the air gently touching your skin . . . Feel the air around your body, noticing the coolness of the breeze as it moves across your face . . . If you are in the woods, notice the freshness of the air around you . . . Listen to the sounds of the forest . . . of birds singing in the trees . . . the wind rustling the leaves . . . Use all your senses to take in the qualities of your environment . . . Continue to sense the air around you . . . What scents do you smell? . . . Now sense the ground beneath you . . . How does it feel? . . . Listen to the sounds around you . . . What do you hear? . . . What does the rest of your body feel? . . . Notice if there is tension anywhere in your body, and relax as you visit this environment . . . Now I will be quiet for a little while. During this time, experience this place for a few minutes. I will call you back shortly . . .* [**Wait three to five minutes.**] *Now begin to gently bring your awareness back to the classroom . . . Keeping your eyes closed, begin to wiggle your toes or stretch your fingers . . . You may want to take a gentle stretch, raising your arms above your head . . . Slowly open your eyes and adjust to the light around you . . . Close your eyes if the light is too bright, and slowly reopen them, each time extending the amount of time your eyes are open . . . Once your eyes are open, take a moment to reacquaint yourself with your surroundings* [**It is important to allow students two to three minutes for this transition.**]

Bibliography and Resources

Works Cited

Achebe, Chinua. 1959. *Things Fall Apart*. New York: Doubleday.

Ackerman, Diane. 1990. *A Natural History of the Senses*. New York: Random House.

Adams, James L. 2001. *Conceptual Blockbusting: A Guide to Better Ideas*. Cambridge, Mass.: Perseus Publishing.

Anderson, Judy. 1996. *Social Contract—What We Believe*. Saskatoon, Saskatchewan: Chelsom Consultants. Available at www.realrestitution.com/orderform.html

Andrews, Ted. 1994. *Animal Speak*. St. Paul, Minn.: Llewellyn Publications.

Arrien, Angeles. 1992. *Signs of Life*. New York: Jeremy P. Tarcher.

Beck, Charlotte Joko. 1989. *Everyday Zen*. San Francisco: Harper San Francisco.

Black Elk, John Gneisenau Neihardt, and Vine Deloria, Jr. 2000. *Black Elk Speaks: Being the Life Story of a Holy Man of the Oglala Sioux*. Greenwich, Conn.: Bison Books.

Brussat, Frederic, and Mary Ann Brussat. 1996. *Spiritual Literacy*. New York: Scribner.

Cameron, Julia. 1992. *The Artist's Way*. New York: Putnam Books.

Campbell, Don. 1997. *The Mozart Effect*. New York: Avon Books.

Cisneros, Sandra. 1989. *The House on Mango Street*. New York: Vintage Books.

Cornell, Judith. 1994. *Mandalas: Luminous Symbols for Healing*. Wheaton, Ill.: Questbooks.

Das, Lama Surya. 1999. *Awakening to the Sacred*. New York: Broadway Books.

David, Marc. 1994. *Nourishing Wisdom: A Mind/Body Approach to Nutrition and Well-Being*. New York: Harmony Books.

De Mello, Anthony. 1991. *The Way of Love*. New York: Doubleday.

Devi, Nischala. 2000. *The Healing Path of Yoga*. New York: Three Rivers Press.

Edwards, Tryon. 1951. *The New Dictionary of Thoughts*. New York: Standard Book Company.

Evans, Robert. 2001. "In the Wake of Crisis: Taking Care of Caretakers." NAIS. Retrieved November 21, 2001, www.humanrelationsservice.org/childrencrisis.html

Fairchild, Kristen. 1997. "Sacred Spaces: An Interview with Jean McMann." Grace. Retrieved November 16, 2001, www.gracecathedral.org/enrichment/interviews/int_19980505.shtml

Fields, Rick, Peggy Taylor, Rex Wheeler, and Rick Ingrasci. 1984. *Chop Wood, Carry Water: A Guide to Finding Spiritual Fulfillment in Everyday Life*. Los Angeles: Jeremy P. Tarcher.

Fincher, Susanne F. n.d. *Sounds True Catalog*. Advertising blurb on *Creating Mandalas*.

Franck, Frederick. 1973. *The Zen of Seeing*. New York: Random House.

Gellman, Rabbi Marc, and Monsignor Thomas Hartman. 1995. *How Do You Spell God?* New York: William Morrow & Company.

Gibson, Clare. 1996. *Signs and Symbols*. New York: Barnes and Noble Books.

Goldman, Johnathan. 2002. *Healing Sounds*. Rochester, Vt.: Healing Arts Press.

Good, E. Perry. 1996. *In Pursuit of Happiness*. Chapel Hill, N.C.: New View Publications.

Gossen, Diane Chelsom. 1996. *Restitution: Restructuring School Discipline*. Chapel Hill, N.C.: New View Publications.

———. 1996. *Restitution Triangle*. Saskatoon, Saskatchewan: Chelsom Consultants. Available at www.realrestitution.com/orderform.html

———. 1999. *Resolving Conflict Using Restitution*. Available at www.realrestitution.com/orderform.html

Halifax, Joan. 1993. *The Fruitful Darkness*. San Francisco: Harper Books.

Hanh, Thich Nhat.1975. *The Miracle of Mindfulness*. Boston: Beacon Press.

———. 1991. *Peace Is Every Step*. New York: Bantam Books.

Hine, Thomas. 2000. *The Rise and Fall of the American Teenager*. New York: HarperPerennial.

Hoff, Benjamin. 1982. *The Tao of Pooh*. New York: Penguin Books.

Horwitz, Claudia. 1999. *A Stone's Throw: Living the Act of Faith*. Durham, N.C.: Stone Circles.

Jung, Carl. 1964. *Man and His Symbols*. New York: Doubleday.

Kempis, Thomas à. 1998. *The Imitation of Christ in Four Books: A Translation from the Latin*. Vintage Spiritual Classics. New York: Vintage Books.

Kessler, Rachael. 2000. *The Soul of Education*. Alexandria, Va.: Association for Supervision and Curriculum Development.

Kesten, Deborah. 2001. "Eating Wisely." (Excerpt from *The Healing Secrets of Food*.) *Yoga Journal* (September/October): 50.

Koch-Sheras, Phyllis R., Amy Lemely, and Peter L. Sheras. 1995. *The Dream Sourcebook and Journal*. New York: Barnes and Noble Books.

Krishnamurti, J. 1953. *Education and the Significance of Life*. San Francisco: HarperCollins.

Lee, Harper. 1960. *To Kill a Mockingbird*. Philadelphia, Pa.: J. B. Lippincott.

Lesser, Elizabeth. 1999. *The New American Spirituality*. New York: Random House.

Lewis, C. S. 1960. *The Four Loves*. New York: Harcourt Brace & Company.

———. 1996. *Mere Christianity*. Nashville, Tenn.: Broadman & Holman.

Libbrecht, Kenneth G. 1999a. "Early Snow Crystal Observations." Retrieved May 25, 2003, from www.its.caltech.edu/~atomic/snowcrystals/earlyobs/earlyobs.htm

———. 1999b. Snowcrystals.net. Retrieved May 25, 2003, from http://www.its.caltech.edu/~atomic/snowcrystals/

Linn, Denise. 1999. *Altars: Bringing Sacred Shrines into Your Everyday Life*. New York: Random House.

McCarthy, Susan, and Jeffrey Moussaieff Masson. 1996. *When Elephants Weep: The Emotional Lives of Animals*. New York: Delta.

McMann, Jean. 1998. *Altars and Icons*. San Francisco: Chronicle Books.

Miller, John P. 2000. *Education and the Soul*. Albany, N.Y.: State University of New York Press.

Morton, Chris. 2001. "The Right of Unbelief." *Teaching Tolerance* (Fall): 48.

Naylor, Gloria. 1998. *The Men of Brewster Place*. New York: Hyperion.

Opoku, Kofi Asare. 1978. *West African Traditional Religion*. Accra, Ghana: FEP International Private Limited.

Pasternak, Boris. 1991. *Doctor Zhivago*. New York: Everyman's Library.

Pearson, Carol S. 1986. *The Hero Within*. San Francisco: Harper San Francisco.

———. 1991. *Awakening the Heroes Within: Twelve Archetypes to Help Us Find Ourselves and Transform Our World*. San Francisco: Harper San Francisco.

Redfield, James. 1997. *The Celestine Prophecy: An Adventure*. New York: Warner Books.

Remarque, Erich Marie. 1995. *All Quiet on the Western Front*. New York: Fawcett Books.

Sark. 1991. *A Creative Companion: How to Free Your Creative Spirit*. Berkeley, Calif.: Celestial Arts.

Secular Humanists. "The Affirmations of Humanism: A Statement of Principles." Retrieved April 30, 2003, www.secularhumanism.org/intro/affirmations.html

Shakespeare, William. 1997. *Macbeth*. London, England: Arden Shakespeare.

———. 1998. *The Tempest*. New York: Signet Classic.

Solzhenitsyn, Alexander. 1998. *One Day in the Life of Ivan Denisovich*. New York: Signet Classic.

Telushkin, Joseph. 1994. *Jewish Wisdom: Ethical, Spiritual, and Historical Lessons from the Great Works and Thinkers*. New York: William Morrow & Company.

Thondup, Tulku. 1996. *The Healing Power of the Mind*. Boston: Shambala.

Thoreau, Henry David, et al. 1982. *The Journal of Henry David Thoreau*. Mineola, N.Y.: Dover Publications.

Wall, Steven, and Harvey Arden. 1990. *Wisdom Keepers: Meetings with Native American Spiritual Elders*. Hillsboro, Ore.: Beyond Words Publishing.

Wiggins, Grant, and Jay McTighe. 1998. *Understanding by Design*. Alexandria, Va.: Association for Supervision and Curriculum Development.

Zahava, Irene. 1988. *Through Other Eyes: Animal Stories by Women*. Berkeley, Calif.: Crossing Press.

Zaleski, Philip. 2000. *The Best Spiritual Writing 2000*. New York: HarperCollins.

Zaleski, Philip, and Paul Kaufman. 1997. *Gifts of the Spirit*. New York: HarperCollins.

Videos and DVDs

Bloomfield, George. 1989. *African Journey*. Goldhil Home Media. [videocassette]

A Force More Powerful: A Century of Non-Violent Conflict. 2000. PBS. [videocassette/DVD] Available for educational/institutional use as six 30-minute video modules. To order, contact Films for the Humanities at 1-800-257-5126, or visit www.films.com.

Johnson, Stephen. 1988. *The Universal Declaration of Human Rights*. Amnesty International, USA. [videocassette] Available to order at http://160.94.193.60/catalog/amnesty.html?menu1= hrrcresources. html&Button1=Go

Krutein, Werner, and David Pomeranz. 1987. *It's In Every One of Us*. New Era Media.

Available for viewing at www.vcsu.edu/vcsutv/channels/spanish/everyone_LAN.html [requires Quicktime player]

Kurosawa, Akira. 2003. *Dreams*. Shido: Warner Home Video. [DVD]

Spielberg, Steven. 1997. *Amistad*. Dreamworks. [videocassette]

Magazines

Faces magazine. Carus Publishing. Available at www.cobblestonepub.com/pages/facemain.htm

New Moon: The Magazine for Girls and Their Dreams. New Moon. Available at www.newmoon.org/magazine/service.htm

Teaching Tolerance. Southern Poverty Law Center. Available at www.tolerance.org/teach/about/index.jsp

Additional Resources

Alexander, Jane. 1999. *Rituals for Sacred Living.* New York: Godsfield Press.

Andrews, Valerie. 1990. *A Passion for This Earth.* San Francisco: HarperCollins.

Bayles, David, and Ted Orland. 1994. *Art and Fear.* Santa Barbara, Calif.: Capra Press.

Borysenko, Joan. 1997. *The Ways of the Mystics.* Carlsbad, Calif.: Hay House.

Carlson, Richard, and Benjamin Shield. 1995. *Handbook of the Soul.* New York: Little, Brown and Company.

Coogan, Michael D. 1998. *The Illustrated Guide to World Religions.* New York: Oxford University Press.

Doe, Mimi, and Marsha Walch. 1998. *10 Principles for Spiritual Parenting.* New York: HarperPerennial.

Fox, James J. 1988. *Indonesian Heritage Religion and Heritage.* Singapore: Archipelago Press.

Ghazi, Suhaib Hamid. 1996. *Ramadan.* New York: Holiday House.

Hope, Jane.1997. *The Secret Language of the Soul.* San Francisco: Chronicle Books.

Kraftsow, Gary. 1999. *Yoga for Wellness.* New York: Penguin.

Lama, Dalai. 1998. *The Art of Happiness.* New York: Riverhead Books.

Levey, Joel, and Michelle Levey.1998. *Living in Balance.* Berkeley, Calif.: Conari Press.

Mislov, Czeslaw. 1988. *The Collected Poems 1931–1987.* New York: Eco Press.

Moore, Thomas. 1998. *Care of the Soul.* New York: HarperCollins.

Rajagopal, D., ed. 1964. *Krishnamurti: Think on These Things.* New York: Harper and Row.

Richards, M.C. 1996. *Opening Our Moral Eye.* Herndon, Va.: Lindisfarne Press.

Russell, Peter. 1992. *Waking up in Time.* Novato, Calif.: Origin Press.

Sullivan, Charles. 1992. *Loving, Poetry and Art.* New York: Harry N. Abrams.

Swan, James A. 1990. *Sacred Places: How the Living Earth Seeks Our Friendship.* Rochester, Vt.: Bear & Co.

About the Authors

Jane Dalton's work as an artist and educator reflects her eclectic experiences. For more than 15 years, Jane has taught all ages and all levels, integrating art and spirituality into the classroom. She earned her MFA from Rochester Institute of Technology's School for American Craftsmen in New York, where she specialized in textile design and weaving. Her love of weaving has taken her throughout South America to study and collect, in addition to extensive travels throughout Europe, Asia, and the United States. The diversity of her personal experiences creates a rich foundation for understanding a variety of cultures and spiritual traditions, which flavor her course content. Jane also received training in human rights education, Spanish language, and art education for grades K through 12.

Jane currently teaches at Warren Wilson College in Asheville, North Carolina. In addition to teaching at the college, she offers inspirational workshops for teachers infused with many of the lessons found in this book. When she is not in the classroom, Jane is busy in her home studio, creating unique works of art that reflect her personal vision. Her work has been exhibited in galleries throughout the United States. Jane practices yoga and meditation and can also be found hiking in the national forests of western North Carolina, or at home in her garden working beside her two cats, Abby and Willow. If you would like more information about Jane, her artwork, and her workshops, visit her website: www.janedalton.com.

Lyn Fairchild has a master's degree in education and a bachelor's degree in English from Stanford University. She has taught English, creative writing, and other humanities courses for over a decade in private and public secondary schools while directing students in dramatic productions, developing student publications, and supporting student initiatives. Lyn has initiated new courses as well as grant-funded programs in service learning, summer enrichment, and other school reforms. She has also served as a gifted education resource teacher and curriculum consultant. Currently, Lyn teaches English at Cary Academy in Cary, North Carolina. During her tenure at Cary Academy, Lyn has earned an Earthwatch Fellowship to assist with archeological study in Ghana and was a 2001 recipient of the All-USA Teacher 3rd Team award and the William Friday Fellowship.

Outside of school, Lyn enjoys singing, acting, creative writing, swing dancing, and writing for an online teacher magazine, *Faculty Shack*. An avid traveler, she also seeks new destinations beyond her past visits to several European and Southeast Asian countries.

Index